ENDOR

insightful spin on two interwoven subjects. Far too often people are either camping in the glory or doing spiritual warfare, but seldom do they understand the relationship between the two. I am refreshed by this teaching and the potential it has to properly equip the next current and emerging generation to live in the glory and to triumph over the enemy!

RYAN LeSTRANGE
Founder of TRIBE, RLM, iHubs
Author of Amazon #1 New Releases *Hell's Toxic Trio*
and *Supernatural Access*

Greater intimacy with God equips and empowers you for deeper levels of spiritual intercession for revival and reformation. Rebecca Greenwood, a seasoned prophetic warrior, captures this principle in *Glory Warfare*, which is filled with Spirit-inspired strategies you can activate and apply in your prayer life. Her experiences and insight on prophetic intercession are powerful and timely for raising up intercessory warriors today. The stories and testimonies will encourage you to grow in your calling and authority as His royal priesthood as you receive biblical impartation of His glory manifest and stand in sync with His Presence, our Champion.

CHÉ AHN
President and Founder, Harvest International Ministry
International Chancellor, Wagner University

Today, the subject of "spiritual warfare" is often made so complex and mystical, it is no wonder many in the modern Church want little to do with it. But not anymore. In *Glory Warfare*, Rebecca Greenwood demystifies spiritual warfare and equips you with surefire devil-defeating strategies. As a believer, you are already assigned for victory, and *Glory Warfare* provides the marching orders to finally possess it.

KYLE WINKLER
Author of *Silence Satan* and *Activating the Power of God's Word*
Creator of the Shut Up, Devil! app
www.kylewinkler.org

There are many spiritual warfare books on the market dealing with some of the same issues Becca does. But this book is fresh; it has life and feels breathed upon by heaven. Not only is the content great but Becca has found a fresh vein of life from which to write about it. I highly recommend this book and also Becca Greenwood!

BARBARA J. YODER
Author of *The Breaker Anointing*
Lead Apostle, Shekinah Regional Apostolic Center

This book, *Glory Warfare*, by my friend, Becca Greenwood, is the much-needed call to strategic worship and intercession for this season of harvest, revival, and world-changing movement of the Holy Spirit that we live in *now!* It is immensely practical, not a lofty conceptual piece but a real-life guide to walk in the glory every day. It will answer many questions for you in your desire to walk in God's glory and what can be accomplished in the heavenlies and on earth as you put this message into practice.

DR. MIKE HUTCHINGS
Director of Education
Global School of Supernatural Ministry,
Global Certification Programs,
and God Heals PTSD Foundation

God is displacing the kingdom of darkness today with His own. He is filling the earth with the knowledge of His glory as the waters cover the sea. Entire nations are being transformed by the power of the gospel and heaven's hosts are engaging satan's who are angry because their time is short.

In *Glory Warfare*, my friend Becca Greenwood transparently allows us into her world. She reveals the secret strategies and techniques that are necessary to win this war. Look over her shoulder as she takes you behind the scenes. Allow her to equip you for battle!

EDDIE SMITH
Author of *Making Sense of Spiritual Warfare*

Here is a book straight from the frontlines of what my late husband C. Peter Wagner called "strategic level warfare." If God calls you to this type of ministry, nothing is more satisfying. And, as Cindy Jacobs says, "The newspaper is your report card." God will honor the effort, and territories will be changed. With the knowledge we now have, we can push back the enemy with great power, and help open an atmosphere conducive for the spreading of the gospel in many needy places on this globe.

Enjoy this exciting book with many stories of personal experiences. Becca and Greg, may your tribe greatly increase in size and geographically so that we take back that which the enemy has stolen all over planet Earth!

"For Yours is the Kingdom, and the Power and the Glory Forever!"

DORIS M. WAGNER
Minister, Glory of Zion and Global Spheres Center, Inc.
Denton, Texas

As I read *Glory Warfare* by Rebecca (Becca) Greenwood, it's easy to see that ministry to the nations is part of her DNA. The first time I saw Becca, I instantly knew the Lord had destined her for great feats in the kingdom. My perception has proved to be true! As her mentor, it has been a joy to watch her anointing increase each year.

From her wealth of knowledge gained from her extensive ministry experiences around the world, Becca exposes the enemy's tools and tactics and explains how consistent, strategic warfare prayer will enable us to achieve more spiritual victories.

Glory Warfare is an easy-to-read reference tool, filled with sound advice, to which you'll return again and again in the days to come. I highly recommend her book to you.

DR. ALICE SMITH
U.S. Prayer Center
Eddie and Alice Ministries
Houston, TX
www.usprayercenter.org

GLORY WARFARE

How the Presence of God
EMPOWERS YOU TO DESTROY THE
WORKS OF DARKNESS

REBECCA
GREENWOOD

DESTINY IMAGE® PUBLISHERS, INC.

P.O. Box 310, Shippensburg, PA 17257-0310

"Promoting Inspired Lives."

This book and all other Destiny Image and Destiny Image Fiction books are available at Christian bookstores and distributors worldwide.

Cover design y Eileen Rockwell
Interior design by Terry Clifton

For more information on foreign distributors, call 717-532-3040.
Reach us on the Internet: www.destinyimage.com.

ISBN 13 TP: 978-0-7684-4325-7
ISBN 13 eBook: 978-0-7684-4326-4
ISBN 13 HC: 978-0-7684-4328-8
ISBN 13 LP: 978-0-7684-4327-1

For Worldwide Distribution, Printed in the U.S.A.
1 2 3 4 5 6 7 8 / 22 21 20 19 18

CONTENTS

FOREWORD

by Chuck D. Pierce

Do we really understand this "Presence-and-Glory War" that is being fought all around us? A better way to approach this may be from an understanding of the atmosphere. According to the *American Dictionary of the English Language,* the atmosphere is the whole mass of fluid, consisting of air, aqueous and other vapors, that surrounds the earth. The word is rooted in the interaction between vapor and the earth's sphere. Vapor consists of the fumes, moist floating substance or invisible elastic fluid that encompasses the earth's sphere. The Bible even refers to this in Psalm 39:5 when it says, *"Certainly every man at his best state is but vapor."* Yet when most of us speak of "the atmosphere," we're referring to a generic sense of an airborne aura surrounding us.

What does the atmosphere have to do with a war over God's presence? In *Glory Warfare,* Becca Greenwood has captured much revelation to help you develop this crucial understanding. We have an atmosphere about us

1

that affects the way the earth operates. The atmosphere we carry affects the land we walk on. The more we are in union with God and His purpose for the earth, the more we create a right atmosphere around us. To usher in God's presence requires a change in the atmosphere, and we are assigned the task of bringing this about! The Bible establishes that satan is the god of this world, the *"prince of the power of the air"* (Eph. 2:2). Yet how is this so if Psalm 24:1 says, *"The earth is the Lord's, and all its fullness"*? First, we must understand the terms used in those two verses. The Greek word for "earth" is *topos*, while the word for "world" is *cosmos*. This means that any structure that protrudes or is above the *topos* is subject to warfare. Second, we must realize the Bible establishes that there are three heavens. God and all His heavenly beings dwell in the third heaven. Satan, as the ruler of the air, attempts to rule from the second heaven to illegally legislate in the first heaven—that place where we physically stand above the earth.

God's manifest presence must be free to rule any particular area of our lives necessary for the fullness of God's destiny to manifest. Once evil is confronted in our atmosphere, then God's presence has the liberty to replace evil with glory. Did you catch that? God's desire is to flood this earth with His glory. Habakkuk 2:14 says, *"For the earth will be filled with the knowledge of the glory of the Lord, as the waters cover the sea."* The thing that prevents God's glory from doing so is the evil in this world, and this is the essence of the presence-and-glory war. There is a fierce war that wages over occupying the atmosphere of this earth. Neighborhoods, cities, regions, nations, continents—each has atmospheric boundaries that have either been declared for the purposes of darkness or for housing God's glory. If we read Habakkuk 2:14 with this understanding, we see that the Lord already has a plan to remove evil that is blocking His presence and glory from invading the entire earth realm. His Word declares that *"the earth **will be** filled"* (emphasis added), which means that the plan of fullness He has for the earth *must be* manifested.

This book is a wonderful read of practical examples and revelatory insights concerning the GLORY WAR that is raging around you. In the midst of our conflicts, we must never forget that God has a plan for our lives. Many times, darkness wants to rule through fear to stop us from entering into the ultimate plan the Lord has for us. We must never forget that His plan is good. We are familiar with the account in Jeremiah 32 in which God asked the prophet to stake his claim on the future by buying a field that was about to go into desolation. In the midst of all the darkness that was surrounding Jerusalem, Jeremiah prophesied that God would eventually restore Israel and Judah, and a remnant would be saved. If we stray from the Lord, He offers a way to bring us back and restore His plan for us. He has a future of prosperity for us. Jeremiah 31:23-33 says:

> *Thus says the Lord of hosts, the God of Israel: "They shall again use this speech in the land of Judah and in its cities, when I bring back their captivity: 'The Lord bless you, O home of justice, and mountain of holiness!' And there shall dwell in Judah itself, and in all its cities together, farmers and those going out with flocks. For I have satiated the weary soul, and I have replenished every sorrowful soul." After this I awoke and looked around, and my sleep was sweet to me. "Behold, the days are coming, says the Lord, that I will sow the house of Israel and the house of Judah with the seed of man and the seed of beast. And it shall come to pass, that as I have watched over them to pluck up, to break down, to throw down, to destroy, and to afflict, so I will watch over them to build and to plant...Behold, the days are coming that I will make a new covenant...not according to the covenant I made with their fathers...but this is the covenant that I will make with the house of Israel...I will put My law in their minds and write on their hearts and I will be their God and they shall be My people" (NKJV).*

Once Jeremiah staked his claim on the future, it really didn't matter that there was darkness that would attempt to overcome his land—because God had a plan. If we trust Him in the midst of our warfare and obey Him to do the faith acts He requires of us, God will secure our future even in the midst of war. Jeremiah 33:3 says, *Call to Me and I will answer you and show you great and mighty things, fenced in and hidden, which you do not know [do not distinguish and recognize, have knowledge of and understand]"* (AMPC). Because God has a great future for us, we can shout loudly and get His attention in the midst of our warfare so that He shows us things we could not normally see. In the midst of whatever haziness presents itself in the now, He will show us our future. Most of us are used to watching out for what we presently have and what is dear to us. But we must also watch after our future.

Glory Warfare helps you to understand the war over your future. This book builds faith! We can neither watch *after* or *for* the future if we do not have the presence of the Lord. It is His presence that allows us to see into our future. Sadly, many Christians get nervous when talking about seeing into the future. We give this the same stigma associated with fortune-tellers and palm readers. Let me say this as clearly as I know how: God's people must have foresight! We must have vision for what lies ahead, or we will be unprepared. And in these times, preparation and readiness is essential. *Glory Warfare* will prepare you for the future. One of the primary reasons God allows us to see into the future is to keep hope of an expected end occurring in the midst of adversity around us. Another reason is for the benefit of the generations who are arising. We must prepare the way for God's best in the lives of those who will follow. The Lord doesn't give us glimpses just to titillate us or make us long for better days ahead. The vision of God—which we all need—always has a divine purpose. Yet another reason God supplies prophetic vision is simply for strategy. We cannot be victorious against the forces of darkness that rule our world without the precise, perfect plans of the Lord.

You will learn much about this as you read this book. The enemy can only mimic the truth. This has always been the case. We find plenty of people in the Bible who were able to predict the future, yet they had aligned themselves with the enemy. How much more, then, is the God of all truth willing to reveal His plans for the future to His own children? Prophecy—which is simply the testimony of Jesus' reign in the coming days—is all about vision. And in the presence of God, there is perfect vision. Habakkuk 2:1-4 says:

> *I will stand my watch and set myself on the rampart, and watch to see what He will say to me, and what I will answer when I am corrected. Then the Lord answered me and said: "Write the vision and make it plain on tablets, that he may run who reads it. For the vision is yet for an appointed time; but at the end it will speak, and it will not lie. Though it tarries, wait for it; because it will surely come, it will not tarry. Behold the proud, his soul is not upright in him; but the just shall live by his faith." (NKJV).*

When we live in the Spirit and see by the Spirit, we gain vision for our future. Not only does God reorder our time, but He positions us in a place so that He can extend the horizon line of heaven and cause us to "see" what He sees. This is what makes us a prophetic people. Acts 17:24-27 says:

> *God, who made the world and everything in it, since He is Lord of heaven and earth, does not dwell in temples made with hands. Nor is He worshiped with men's hands, as though He needed anything, since He gives to all life, breath, and all things. And He has made from one blood every nation of men to dwell on all the face of the earth, and has determined their preappointed times and the boundaries of their dwellings, so that they should seek the Lord, in the hope that they might*

grope for Him and find Him, though He is not far from each one of us (NKJV).

When we are at the right place at the right time, the Lord "pro-horizons" us, or extends our horizon line so that we can see farther than ever before. We are not a people limited to the finite space that we are in. We are a people filled with vision. We can *sense* His presence, *feel* His presence, *see* His presence, and *move in* His presence.

As I mentioned before, God has promised to cover the earth with His glory (see Hab. 2:14). I believe this was His original intent when He planted a Garden and gave it to the human race. He wanted us to cultivate that garden and live in communion with Him so that He could give us a vision of how to effectively invade the whole earth with His presence. However, when we listened to the enemy, our perfect communion was broken with God and our vision became hindered. The same principle applies today. If we adhere to the plans of satan rather than listening to God's voice, we limit God's presence from moving through us and increasing our boundaries. Because of this, there is a huge war raging over His presence. The enemy does all he can to prevent us from seeing what the Lord wants us to see. Satan longs for us not to have vision for our future. Remember, without a vision, we perish (see Prov. 29:18). Let vision arise within you as you read this book. See His glory! *Enter your war ahead with a mind to triumph! Glory Warfare* will build up your faith and help develop your thought processes of triumph in every conflict you face in days ahead.

DR. CHUCK D. PIERCE
President, Glory of Zion International Ministries
President, Global Spheres, Inc.

INTRODUCTION

by Cindy Jacobs

It seems that the need for good teaching on the subject of spiritual warfare is critical for our times more than ever before. Becca Greenwood's new book, *Glory Warfare*, is one of the best I have read.

In a conversation with the late C. Peter Wagner, we both agreed that there was a whole generation that had not learned to do spiritual warfare. This, in some ways, has left people, both in their personal lives and in their job, to pray for their nations to be discipled and taught of the Lord, unequipped to pray on a strategic level that pierces the darkness that demonic powers have amassed.

Glory Warfare fills this gap.

There are a number of reasons why I say this:

First of all, it is new and fresh. God has been speaking to many prophetic leaders about God's release of fresh waves of glory into the earth realm. Many people do not have knowledge of how to use the position of warring from the throne room of God down rather than our human knowledge up. This book does that for the reader.

Second, because Becca is not simply a theoretician but a practitioner of spiritual warfare, it is practical. She writes from the background of having led strategic prayer teams from Spain to China. She knows what works and this comes out in the pages of the book.

Third, it's transformational! After studying this manual, you will be able to apply what you read to the landscape of your life. You will be able to go from living a defeated life to one of victory.

I want to encourage you to read through the following pages and highlight it as you go because you will want to go back and reference it over and over again.

You are about to have your life changed.

Dr. Cindy Jacobs
Generals International

INTRODUCTION

*Arise, shine, for your light has come, and the glory of the
Lord has risen upon you. For the darkness shall cover the
earth and deep darkness the peoples; but the Lord shall rise
upon you, and His glory shall be seen upon you. The nations
shall come to your light and kings to the brightness of your
rising. Lift up your eyes all around, and see: They all gather
themselves together; they come to you; your sons shall come
from afar, and your daughters shall be carried at your side.
Then you shall see and be radiant, and your heart shall
thrill and rejoice because the abundance of the sea shall be
converted to you, the wealth of the nations shall come to you.*
—ISAIAH 60:1-5

Have you ever considered the possibility that God has chosen to anoint us
in His throne room, in His glory realm to be used mightily by Him to see
peoples and nations set free and transformed? It is my hope and prayer that

through the pages of this book your answer to this question will come to agree with mine. And my answer is an absolute and resounding yes.

Jesus stated, "If I cast out demons by the Spirit of God, surely the kingdom of God has come upon you" (Matt. 12:28 NKJV). A kingdom has a government led by a king. Jesus was the occupying King. The kingdom He waged war against also had a government, with satan as its king. Since the fall of Adam and Eve in the garden, humankind was under the evil dominion of the prince of darkness. Basically, satan could do anything he wanted to the peoples of the earth. He was up to no good. Satan has never nor will he ever play fair. He is complete evil; our adversary; the great deceiver; the enemy of our souls; the prince of the power of air; and the mocking, prideful, rebellious foe of our Lord. But things radically changed when God sent His Son and He made a way for salvation and redemption for all mankind and creation. He positioned those who believe in Him as ones who have access to go beyond the veil into His throne room.

I believe we will all agree that darkness is increasing and satan is sounding out a deafening roar as a ravaging lion looking for prey to devour. That being said, I have also heard it said by many in the Body of Christ that they want nothing to do with spiritual warfare. And many in the Church refuse to even acknowledge that we are in a battle. This exact stance, in essence, tells the enemy that he has already won the battle. The truth is, once we are saved we are enrolled in the most powerful army of the universe, and it is time that we act like it. And friends, we have not been left to fight on our own.

The Word of God repeatedly discloses the power encounters Jesus had with satan and his army of darkness. The Bible reports that the very first encounter that happened to Jesus after God audibly announced, "This is My beloved Son, in whom I am well pleased," was that "Jesus was led up... into the wilderness to be tempted by the devil" (Matt. 3:17; 4:1 NKJV). C. Peter Wagner pointedly states: "Jesus's public ministry began with an eyeball to eyeball power encounter with satan himself!"[1]

In the real world, Jesus talked about, taught about, and personally confronted the devil and the demons under his command regularly. When the apostle John looked back at the ministry of Jesus, he characterized it in this way: "For this purpose the Son of God was manifested, that He might destroy the works of the devil" (1 John 3:8 NKJV). From the time of Jesus until now, the battle has intensified and continues to intensify. Satan's fury is raging because he knows his time is short. There is an army of spiritual warriors God is raising up to partner with Him in the final defeat and demise of the evil foe—satan and his kingdom of darkness. You and I, as sons and daughters of the heavenly King, have been given the privileged position of enlisted warriors of this heavenly appointed army.

You see, when we encounter our King in the glory of His throne room, when we ascend into His presence, we become awakened ones. Scriptures tells us, "He who is faithful in what is least is faithful also in much" (Luke 16:10 NKJV). As we faithfully enter His glory realm and encounter Him, we move from acquaintance, to awakened ones, to friends, to trust, to intimates, to glory-empowered Kingdom ambassadors. Our hearts are vitally united to His and set aflame with His Kingdom purposes. The more time we spend in these heavenly encounters where we are surrounded and empowered in His glory, the better we know Him and His voice. He entrusts us with strategies to release, intercede, prophesy, decree, and implement so that the powerful light of His Kingdom is made known, causing darkness to be dispelled and evil to flee. The Holy Spirit deposits in each of us a distinct sound that comes from the roar of the lion of Judah that sets captives free and awakens cities and nations, ushering them into transformational breakthrough.

I would like to share a recent prophetic revelation the Lord released from a glory encounter with Him while I was in intercession late into the night hours for our nation and the nations.

In the midst of all the storms, the chaos, the stirred-up tensions there is a sound that is arising from My bride, the Ekklesia. It is a distinct sound rising in a unified composition being played before My throne and echoing throughout the land and the nation and nations.

There is a sound of the groans of intercession, a sound of crying in total dependence and abandonment to our heavenly Father. The Father of the universe and all creation. A sound of a groaning in the spirit over the land and coming from the land. It is not a sound of death, but a sound of holiness, consecration, hope, and life that is designed by our Father in Heaven. A season of pressing through a narrow place and coming through the eye of the needle into a place of His designed Kingdom purpose and destiny. Even though the flood waters have risen, the fires have burned, cities and nations have trembled and quaked—there is a crying out. An awakening that is sweeping this nation. An awakening of believers, intercessors, prayer warriors. A united strength that all felt was lost is now being ignited, rediscovered, rebirthed, and released.

It is the sound of an awakened prayer army—My Ekklesia. There is a new sound of surrender, repentance, dependence on Him. A sound of intercession of awakening that only comes from the surrendered bowing of the knee and the laying prostrate in His glorious presence of the throne room. It is that place where we can only imagine how magnificent He is, but still experience and encounter Him in His awesome glory. It is a sound of worship and awakening. A sound of the warriors arising. A sound and a stirring of an authoritative rising up! A warrior's cry of authority is resounding out into the atmosphere. It is a sound and a display of unity.

There is a culminating voice of unity arising in a remnant that is on the horizon of being expressed that many thought had been silenced and divided. While the chaos comes to a fullness of expression, the sound of this new, repentant, humbled, empowered army is rising from the land to the heavenlies.

Yes, chaos is raising its head for a set time, yet the sounds arising from the awakened intercession and Ekklesia will increase. It will in time overpower the sound of chaos. Hold fast to the Lord. Keep your abiding gaze focused intently on Him. Rise up! Now is not the time to be dormant or complacent. Take those action steps He is asking you to take. Press into Him. He is a good, good Father. Jesus is the victorious King.

ENTER THE GLORY REALM

*As air is the atmosphere of the earth, glory is
the atmosphere of Heaven. It lifts us up above
the earthly, into the very presence of God.*
—RUTH WARD HEFLIN,
Glory: Experiencing the Atmosphere of Heaven

GLORY. We have heard statements such as, "He is glorious!" "Lord, bring Your glory." "What a powerful service; the glory was strong." I myself have even made these comments. Allow me to pose a question. What does this word actually mean? The Hebrew word for glory is *kabod*. It is splendor, honor, wealth, manifestation of power, glorious presence, reward, glory in the inner person, ruler, men of high rank, one who governs (Strong's #H3519). As stated in Isaiah 4:5, "Then the Lord will create upon every dwelling place of Mount Zion, and upon her assemblies, a cloud and smoke by day and the shining of a flaming fire by night. For over all the glory shall be a covering." In this context it becomes a covering, which is a defense, canopy, shelter from the elements, and bridal chamber. It also comes as the Shekinah glory, which is the manifest weight and heaviness of the Lord. We must not mention the glory without speaking of the time when the glory fell so strongly in the temple that the priests could not stand nor perform their duties.

> *The priests then left the Holy Place. All the priests there were consecrated, regardless of rank or assignment; and all the Levites who were musicians were there—Asaph, Heman, Jeduthun, and their families, dressed in their worship robes; the choir and orchestra assembled on the east side of the Altar and were joined by 120 priests blowing trumpets. The choir and trumpets made one voice of praise and thanks to God— orchestra and choir in perfect harmony singing and playing praise to God:*
>
> *Yes! God is good!*
>
> *His loyal love goes on forever!*
>
> *Then a billowing cloud filled The Temple of God. The priests couldn't even carry out their duties because of the cloud—the glory of God!—that filled The Temple of God* (2 Chronicles 5:13-14 MSG).

It is beautiful reality that the Lord has designed for us to encounter. I will always remember the first time I saw an overwhelming presence of the Lord's glory, a glory cloud that literally descended upon and enveloped hundreds of people in a very dramatic way. It was in the early 1990s. The church we were attending was on the verge of an all-out revival. Oftentimes, services would continue until two to three in the afternoon. No one allowed weekend plans to interfere with attending a Sunday evening service because missing a service most assuredly meant missing a move of God. As we gathered corporately, the Lord was faithful to move in tangible and glorious ways.

One particular evening, I was singing on the worship team. That night when we arrived for practice prior to the service, the weight of His presence entered into the sanctuary. Rehearsal never ended. In a place of surrender we continued to exalt Him. As members arrived and entered the room, they instantly responded to His presence and quietly made their way to a seat or the altar. No one had to explain His glory was there. All who entered immediately knew. We had entered the glory realm, the realm of eternity. The realm of the revelation of the presence of God. At one point as we continued in abandoned worship, the weight was heavy and unearthly, beyond human words of expression. I opened my eyes to see. As I looked out over the crowd, I watched as a thick cloud supernaturally descended on hundreds of people. No eyes were opened. Each person was lost in the moment with the Lord. Suddenly, without anyone in the congregation aware of what the others were doing, each person in that sanctuary in full abandonment raised their hands simultaneously, threw their heads back, opened their eyes, and began to shout, "Jesus! Jesus! Jesus!" People fell out in the presence, weeping, and joy broke out across the auditorium. Jesus had entered that room that night. Lives were radically transformed. Many were set free and several saved.

He is glory. When we encounter Him in that glory realm of the throne room of heaven it is transforming. Paul shares in Second Corinthians 3:17-18: "Now the Lord is the Spirit, and where the Spirit of the Lord is, there is liberty [emancipation from bondage, true freedom]. And we all, with unveiled face, continually seeing as in a mirror the glory of the Lord, are progressively being transformed into His image from [one degree of] glory to [even more] glory, which comes from the Lord, [who is] the Spirit" (AMP). God not only wants us set free, He wants us to find that freedom by encountering Jesus in His perfect, glorious, kingly majesty so that we will become the reflection of His resplendent, divine brightness. Friends, I can attest to the truth that when we draw near to Jesus and encounter

Him personally in all His majestic holiness, He draws near to us and His light and love transform us. When that takes place, nothing and no one can ever take from us that supernatural, glorious, transformational moment. It becomes a defining moment in our lives, one that affirms who we are and what we have become—people captivated by Jesus and abandoned to the Father, spiritually on fire for Him and totally committed to Him from a place of deep, sincere thankfulness.

From this place of transformational personal encounter, our hearts continue to stir and a hunger is ignited as we draw nearer and nearer to Him. Friends, He is a relational Father and He desires for each of us to cultivate an atmosphere to experience more of Him. Not only to experience more of Him, but to enter into a place in the heavenly throne room beyond the veil. When Jesus died on the cross, the veil to the holy of holies was rent in two from top to bottom. This signified that Jesus had now made a way for all mankind, for those who would choose Him and His Kingdom, to have access to Him and His glorious presence. What is even more profound and beautiful is that He sent the Holy Spirit to be here with us to anoint and empower all believers to walk in a supernatural life. John the Baptist clearly states in Luke 3:16 what Jesus will bring: "But John intervened: 'I'm baptizing you here in the river. The main character in this drama, to whom I'm a mere stagehand, will ignite the Kingdom life, a fire, the Holy Spirit within you, changing you from the inside out. He's going to clean house—make a clean sweep of your lives. He'll place everything true in its proper place before God; everything false he'll put out with the trash to be burned'" (MSG). To understand more fully what occurred at Pentecost and what is available to each of us today, let's look at what we receive when we welcome the infilling of the Holy Spirit.

HOLY SPIRIT EMPOWERED

"Suddenly a sound like a mighty rushing wind came from heaven, and it filled the whole house where they were sitting" (Acts 2:2). For some reason, in my own thinking I always knew this event was significant, but I never fully understood or grasped how incredibly supernatural this historic encounter was until three years ago in an all-night intercession time. In the early morning hours, the Lord led me to study the full meaning of the words from Acts 2:1-4 and to do so from the Bible software I use when studying and preparing teachings. Suffice it to say that this event in the Upper Room was not casual. And while receiving the gift of tongues is awesome and I am so blessed to have a prayer language, this was only a portion of what transpired for the 120 disciples and what is made available to each of us.

When studying the translation of the words *mighty rushing wind*, a clear and descriptive picture of what happened is established. This wind was mighty and it carried a force, impact, and burden. As it rushed in, it went to the very deepest part of a man or woman that is able to respond to God. They were suddenly, instantly filled with the very breath of life of God Himself, the Holy Spirit. And when they were filled, their minds, thoughts, emotions, and belief in spirit-realm encounters were instantaneously transformed into a new paradigm and a Kingdom of God way of thinking. It was a sudden and drastic change that filled each of them with boldness, joy, and fire, and tongues of fire were distributed on each of them. The fire of the Holy Spirit anointed and empowered each of them and they were set aflame, a burning torch. Let's depict this in an even clearer picture. Instead of looking at the burning bush, they became the burning bush. The burning ones, commissioned by God Himself to go out and boldly proclaim the Gospel, to see a harvest come forth and to literally carry an empowerment to dramatically turn the world upside down for the Kingdom of God. The Holy Spirit is this wind—the very breath of God, the fire carrying the glory and His *ruach*, His breath of life that comes into the deepest part of a man or woman who can respond to Him. Just as the 120 were filled, we too are completely filled, transformed from the inside out, and emboldened with His fire and glory to move and advance His Kingdom in this lost world.

Holy Spirit is God here with us. When we are baptized in Him and cultivate a relationship with Him, there is a power and authority given to pray to see breakthrough come. He fills us with His fire and presence. He ushers us into the throne room to encounter Jesus and His glory. In this place we are awakened to the reality that we are vitally united to Jesus and our heavenly Father and empowered and anointed for great Kingdom exploits. Our spiritual eyes and ears are open to see and hear as Jesus speaks and leads us in our intercession. We are filled with the might and power of Jesus—a light that causes darkness to be expelled. Boldness, power, and authority are realized to engage in effective warfare to see victory. Some reading might be praying faithfully but are not seeing results or breakthrough in your intercession. I want to speak encouragement that if you have not received the infilling of the Holy Spirit, invite Him into your life. Welcome Him to baptize you in His glorious presence. As you cultivate a relationship with Him, His power and authority for victory will be ignited and made known in your intercession.

Another transformational promise in this encounter—the Holy Spirit "filled the whole house where they were sitting." The *whole house* meant the room, each person in that room, a temple or meeting place of the Lord, the entire family line from generation to generation, and the property and possessions associated with a house or household (Strong's #G3624). Meaning that the family line is now marked to have the choice to receive this awesome gift! Wow! What an awesome prayer strategy when praying for our family, prodigals, and our homes and possessions—praying from the promise of the blessing that is placed on our family line when we are filled with the Spirit of God.

> *Lord, cause the prodigals to hear and feel the wooing and nudging of Your Spirit so that they will respond to Your pull in the Spirit to return to You. Lord, we say in all areas where our*

lost loved ones and friends have struggled in a battle to know Your truth, that they will hear and respond to Your voice, Your Spirit, and be saved. We prophesy this in agreement with the promise that You have marked our family lines to hear and receive You. Let all darkness hear the promise of the Lord. My family will be saved!

PERSONALLY ENTERING THE GLORY REALM

We are all familiar with the temple of the Lord so vividly described in the Old Testament. The outer court, the inner chamber, the Holy of Holies that housed the Ark of the Covenant, the very presence of God. The blueprint of the temple was a picture that the God we worship is a Trinity. Three persons in one—Father, Son, and Holy Spirit. The Word of God tells us we are made in His image and likeness, and we are three-part beings made up of the body, soul, and spirit. Just as the temple was modeled on God's design of a three-person Trinity, Father, Son and Holy Spirit, the divine forming and make-up of each of us is that, we too, are the temple— body, soul, and spirit. When Jesus came, He made the way for each of us to be anointed and appointed in the throne room of His presence.

As previously discussed, the veil was rent in two. The Holy Spirit is the heavenly host within the inner chambers of the Holy of Holies. He prepares and serves our spiritual food. He lifts us up into the presence of Jesus into His throne room to encounter Him in His glory. The fire, glory, and presence that was depicted in the temple in the Old Testament within the Holy of Holies is now within each of us. As ones who are a new creation in Christ filled with the Holy Spirit, we become the carriers of His fire and glory—the living temples of the Lord. This is the dimension in which everything in our Christian walk is to be birthed.

Friends, as we advance in this teaching it will be made evident that this is where the assignments for warfare are spoken and the blueprint strategies for victory revealed. We then bring the blueprints we have received and implement them in the earth to possess the land for Him. In other words, we bring heaven to earth. So how do we begin to experience, activate, and walk out this spiritual truth?

ABIDE IN HIM

> *Dwell in Me, and I will dwell in you. [Live in Me and I will live in you.] Just as no branch can bear fruit of itself without abiding in (being vitally united to) the vine, neither can you bear fruit unless you abide in Me* (John 15:4 AMPC).

> *If you live in Me [abide vitally united to Me] and My words remain in you and continue to live in your hearts, ask whatever you will, and it shall be done for you* (John 15:7 AMPC).

Ask whatever you will and it will be done for you? Wow, what a promise. But some might be asking, "Is hhe saying God answers whatever we ask of Him?" My answer is yes and no. It depends on the basis and the foundation where the intercession and prayer originated. Allow me to explain further.

Upon hearing the word *abide*, our minds quickly go to the normal steps we have been taught and know to be true, which we will also discuss in depth in this book. However, as we begin to move in that direction, let's take a closer look at this word, *abide*. The Greek word is *meno*. It means to remain, dwell, continue, endure, not to depart from, to continue to be present (continually), to be held and kept (Strong's #G3306). In other words, when we abide we become so in tune with His presence from the dedicated times of entering in beyond the veil and encountering Him in His glory that we grow into the ability to remain in existence with Him. We know who we are in Him. He is very real and close to us. We are not separate or apart, but vitally united to. The following is an incredible promise that Jesus shared:

No one has greater love [no one has shown stronger affection] than to lay down (give up) his own life for his friends. You are My friends if you keep on doing the things which I command you to do. I do not call you servants (slaves) any longer, for the servant does not know what his master is doing (working out). But I have called you My friends, because I have made known to you everything that I have heard from My Father. [I have revealed to you everything that I have learned from Him.] You have not chosen Me, but I have chosen you and I have appointed you [I have planted you], that you might go and bear fruit and keep on bearing, and that your fruit may be lasting [that it may remain, abide], so that whatever you ask the Father in My Name [as presenting all that I AM], He may give it to you (John 15:13-16 AMPC).

Such an awesome Kingdom promise. He is stating that you and I can be vitally united to Him, His friends to whom He reveals everything, and we will see answers to our prayers. I believe He hears all of our prayers. But the key is this—when we are vitally united to Him our prayer burdens and assignments become those that He has entrusted to us. Praying in unison and agreement with His heart over a matter is key for breakthrough. Truthfully, to be vitally united to Him and effectual intercessors, warriors, prophets, and believers, we must know the realms of the glory. Otherwise we live in the realm of man's understanding and spend most of our time interceding and warring over all the wrong things. When we move in beyond the veil into the realm of His Spirit. He shows us what to target because the glory causes our spiritual eyes and ears to be opened to see, hear, and receive from Him. Therefore, we must be intentional of pursuing Him so our spiritual walk and intercession becomes His intercession and we see the breakthrough come.

SET ASIDE TIME WITH HIM

Time spent in prayer will yield more than that given to work. Prayer alone gives work its worth and its success. Prayer opens the way for God to do His work in us and through us. Let our chief work as God's messengers be intercession: in it we secure the presence and power of God to go with us.

—ANDREW MURRAY, *The Ministry of Intercession*

In intercession our King upon His throne finds His Highest glory; in it we will find our highest glory too.

—ANDREW MURRAY, *The Plea for More Prayer*

Drawing close to Him is essential. You must have a time and place that provides an uninterrupted atmosphere to focus on Him. For some, this might be hours. The location should be one where you are not interrupted by phone calls, texts, social media, television, other people, or anything that will distract. This is a committed space and time just between you and Him. This is about building relationship. As beautifully stated by Alice Smith, "He has rent the veil, but we must open the door! We must risk being known completely if we are to be complete in Him."[1] Hear me. It is my prayer that as you read this book this reality awakens you—He desires to commune with you, to have relationship with you, and for you to encounter Him in His glory. The more we allow and make room for this time, the more our ability to yield to the Spirit and flow in His anointing and presence increases. Therefore, when we are called to wield authority in the Spirit we hit the mark and see results.

ASCENDING THROUGH PRAISE, THANKSGIVING, AND WORSHIP

Praise until the spirit of worship comes. Worship until the glory comes. Then stand in the glory.

—RUTH WARD HEFLIN,
Glory: Experiencing the Atmosphere of Heaven

There is a progression that occurs when we enter into His presence through praise, thanksgiving, and worship. Praise Him for who He is. Exalt Him and speak His greatness. In this dedicated, set-aside time, don't come with a list of problems to repeat and pray through. The more we do this and longer we do this, the more our faith begins to waver. Why? Because the problem grows bigger and bigger and we will not ascend into His throne room to receive from Him. Make this allotted time about Him and glorify Him in His goodness and greatness. He delights in our praise. Our voice is the greatest instrument of praise that the Lord has given us.

Praise, worship, and glorify our heavenly Father, Jesus, and the Holy Spirit. They are three persons in one, each with their own personality and desire to relate to us. Therefore, all should be exalted and intimacy developed with all three. Praise is just the beginning. We continue on in this journey of glorifying His character, holiness, love, and majesty and we enter into worship. Allow me to share, at this point, that sometimes we sell ourselves short by not crossing over the finish line. What do I mean by this? We settle for a taste of Him or an increased anointing, but He wants us to continue until we encounter His glory. Press through into abandoned and surrendered encounters until our praise rises with the sound of thundering and echoing into the atmosphere, as John so clearly heard: "the voice of a great multitude," "the voice of many waters," and "the voice of mighty thunderings" (Rev. 19:6 KJV). Praise releases the atmosphere for victory; worship releases the atmosphere for His presence and anointing, which usher us into the throne room of His glory.

He Is Not Threatened by Our Imperfections

As we will discuss in Chapter Three, His love is unconditional. You can bring your flaws, failures, and concerns into His presence; and when you are in that face-to-face glory presence, His goodness, loving-kindness, and love will bring you to a point of cleansing and forgiveness as you submit yourself to Him.

In this place of abiding, it will produce:

1. Purity: The more time we spend in His presence, the more we become like Him and are transformed into His image.

2. Revelation: Time in His presence causes us to learn His voice and to know His ways. Revelation, wisdom, and prophecy increase and accuracy is developed. And we will pray, prophesy, and decree as He directs.

3. A surrender to His ways and a life of obedience: Abiding births a hunger causing us to want to rise to a position of remaining vitally united to Him through a life of obedience to His voice and leadings.

4. A willingness to die to ourselves: Our focus becomes about Him and His Kingdom as we allow Him to do a deep work in our lives. A cry of personal transformation and change begins to resonate through us, "Lord, I want more of You! I am hungry for more of You! Because there is so much more. Lord, I want to know You more!"

5. Humility: We remain low in order rise up.

6. Discernment: Time in His presence and Word and gleaning from His truths will cause sensitivity and discernment. The ability to know good from evil, right from wrong. A knowing when He has entered the room, when the angelic realm is with us, and when evil is present. A knowing and discerning of the times we are in.

7. Strategies and blueprints for breakthrough to glory-anointed prayer assignments: These assignments that carry an anointing for victory cause darkness to fear, tremble, and flee.

8. Authority: As we posture ourselves before Him there is a rising up that occurs in our spirit to stand, intercede, contend, and partner with Him to see His Kingdom manifested in the world.

The more you spend time with Him in the glory, the more you will begin to radiate Him. Moses is a great example. He spent 40 days abiding in the spiritual glory realm. When he descended from that mountain, the glory was so visible on him that he had to wear a veil. Time of abiding in the glory will be made known and evident. Personal revival is moving beyond the anointing and abiding in His glory. People and the spiritual realm will see it on you and hear it in your voice. It will resound with an awakened sound in your praise and worship. The glory marks people in a distinct way for the Kingdom of God.

Rees Howells: Abiding to Bind the Strongman

The following is a testimony of one of the most powerful anointed intercessors who influenced world history with undeniable, measurable results. His name was Rees Howells. It was actually during the time of reading the book *Rees Howells Intercessor* by Norman Grubb that I experienced incredible supernatural glory encounters with Jesus in which He spoke to me with clear certainty the calling to intercession in the nations. Let's learn from Mr. Howells' journey how we too can abide to victory and breakthrough.

One night, when Rees Howells and his friends were returning from the villa, they passed a group of women who never came to their meetings. They could tell by their voices that they had been drinking. One of the party exclaimed, "Where is the power to change these people?" It was a challenge, and Rees Howells took it. There and then the Spirit gave it to him that he was to pick out the ringleader of those women, who was a notorious character and a confirmed drunkard, and pray her into the Kingdom by Christmas Day!

Allow me to pause here and ask this question: When we are presented with challenges such as this, do we shrink back, or do we accept it and stand? You see, the Holy Spirit spoke to him that he was to accept the challenge, abide, stand, and believe, and by Christmas day this woman would be saved. In accepting this challenge, he received clear instructions that he was not to do it by personally speaking with her about the Gospel. He was to win her salvation in the abiding place of the throne room.

For Rees this was a new place of intercession. He had seen many bound by alcohol receive salvation, but it had always been through personal connections. In this particular situation, he did not know this woman. The Lord was using this to cause his faith in the place of abiding to grow. It was a test of strength to obediently follow the Lord's leading and press into the power of atonement through Jesus' death and resurrection. He was to bind the strongman and see his house plundered in this woman's life through this abiding place. Once he saw this victory, he would be able to see it and apply it over many other prayer burdens to affect many.

As we continue to look at this testimony, ask the Lord to open your spiritual understanding to hear and receive His prayer strategies for breakthrough. Sometimes we are presented with challenges that seem difficult. More times than not, the Lord's strategy will seem unconventional to our own way of thinking. But when we are obedient to come into His abiding place and hear His blueprint plan for breakthrough and pray accordingly, we witness Him move in glorious ways. Let's continue to learn of the victorious outcome this abiding place secured for this woman.

The Spirit gave him John 15:7: "If ye abide in Me, and My words abide in you, ye shall ask what ye will, and it shall be done unto you." It would all depend on his abiding.

As this "abiding" was to take such a central place in his future life of intercession, it is important to see what the Holy Spirit taught Mr. Howells about it. The key text, John 15:7, makes it plain that the promise is unlimited, but its fulfillment would depend on the abiding. That is why in all cases of intercession, Mr. Howells constantly spoke of guarding his "place of abiding."

The Scriptural key to abiding is in 1 John 2:6, "He that saith he abideth in Him ought himself also to walk even as He walked." In other words, it meant being willing for the Holy Spirit to live through him the life the Savior would have lived if He had been in his place.: "The one who says he abides in Him ought himself to walk in the same manner as He walked" (NASB).

The way Mr. Howells maintained the abiding was by spending a set time of waiting upon God every day during the period in which the intercession lasted. The Holy Spirit would speak to him through the Word, revealing any standard that he was to come up to, particularly in "the laws of the Kingdom"—Sermon on the Mount. Any command the Spirit gave him, he must fulfill because the abiding is the keeping of His commandments (John 15:10). The Spirit would also search his heart and throw light on his daily life, revealing any motives or actions that needed confession and cleansing in the Blood.

The Spirits dealing were not so much with outward shortcomings as with the self-nature out of which they sprang. Any transgression was never to be repeated, but specific obedience on that point would be called for until radical inward change was effected. He was "purified...in obeying the truth through the Spirit" (1 Peter 1:22).

The necessity for abiding is seen in that same chapter—John 15. The life is the Vine. As the branch remains united to it by abiding in it, that life of the Vine produces the fruit through the branch. In other words, the power is in Christ. As the intercessor remains united to Him by abiding in Him, His power operates through the intercessor and accomplishes what needs to be done.

As Mr. Howells would continue in this place of abiding day by day he would be increasingly conscious that the Spirit was engaging the enemy in battle and overcoming him, until finally he would become fully assured of the victory. The Spirit would then tell him that the intercession was finished, the position gained, and he would await the visible deliverance in praise and faith.

There are degrees and stages in abiding. The deeper the oneness, the more the power of the risen life of Christ can operate through the channel, and new positions of spiritual authority be gained...But with obedience came cleansing, until by the second week, he said, "I had become more used to my position, and could see the Holy Ghost binding the devil. I soon realized I was not fighting against flesh and blood, but 'against wicked spirits in heavenly places.'"

The weeks that followed, as he "gave prompt obedience to the Holy Spirit in all things," were times of wonderful fellowship, until by the end of the sixth week the Spirit told him the abiding was complete and the victory assured. "I was abiding now without being called to abide, walking in the position, and the Lord told me that I could now expect to see this woman make the move."

That very night, with a thrill in his soul, Rees saw her in the open-air meeting for the first time, and he told the devil, "Now I know the Holy Ghost is stronger than you; you have been brought to nought on Calvary."

He took no steps to influence this woman in any way, but soon she began to come to cottage meetings. A great number of people became onlookers as they heard of the prayer. It was now the case of praising before the victory, and in the remaining weeks before Christmas the Holy Spirit did not allow him to pray for her. "It was a conflict with not praying," he said, "as the adversary pressed on us the need of prayer; but it would have been a prayer of doubt," During that time there was no outward sign of repentance in the woman.

Christmas morning came...When the time for the meeting came, the woman was there, but a lot of people had brought their children; there was plenty of noise, and in no sense the kind of atmosphere which would influence a person to repent. But in the middle of the meeting "down she went on her knees and cried to God for mercy. It was a victory beyond value, and she is standing today."[2]

BRINGING HEAVEN HERE ON EARTH

Even as I type this powerful testimony I weep. Lord, cause me to yield even more to Your Spirit. Holy Spirit, live through me. Cause me to carry the burdens of intercession for my family, my city, my region, my nation, and the nations. Friends, when we encounter Him in the glory realm, we in turn bring heaven here on earth. It is in supernatural abiding encounters in the glory where we are anointed and receive strategies to see the schemes of the enemy defeated, victories won, breakthrough manifested, and transformation made known in the earth. And as prophetically revealed in Habakkuk 2:14, "The earth will be filled with the knowledge of the glory of the Lord."

ENROLLED IN THE MOST POWERFUL ARMY IN THE UNIVERSE

We are on slippery ground. Only intercession will avail.
God is calling for intercessors—men and women who
will lay their lives on the altar to fight the devil.
—REES HOWELLS, *Intercessor*

What Mr. Howells is referring to in the above quote is what is termed spiritual warfare prayer. Spiritual warfare is defined as a power confrontation in the invisible realm between the Kingdom of God and the kingdom of darkness. Many believers have expressed to me their hesitancy to acknowledge spiritual warfare and feel strongly about having no involvement in spiritual battles. My response: "Are you a believer?" The normal reply is, "Yes, I am a Christian and have been for quite some time." My answer usually comes as a surprise: "Well, friend, it is too late! Once we are saved, we are enrolled in the most powerful army in the universe and its time that we act like it!"

It is time for the Church to understand and to confidently carry ourselves as people in the army of God's Kingdom. While some might not be looking for a battle, the devil does not oblige this stance. He has never nor will he ever play fair, and whether we like it or not he has initiated war against us. The truth is the battle began long before you and I arrived on the scene. Satan and his army of darkness hate our heavenly Father as proven in the rebellion. Our Father created us because He desired sons and daughters of His own. As parents, what is the hardest battle to cope with? When our children are struggling and suffering. Our heavenly Father loves each of us in the same manner, but even more than mere human words can fathom. Therefore, in seasons when we are in a battle the enemy is attempting to hurt us and also our Father and His Kingdom by coming against each of us, His sons and daughters, the apple of His eye. As stated so clearly in First Peter 5:8, "Keep a cool head. Stay alert. The Devil is poised to pounce, and would like nothing better than to catch you napping" (MSG).

THE SPIRIT REALM IS ETERNAL

The Bible tells us, "While we look not at the things which are seen, but at the things which are not seen; for the things which are seen are temporal, but the things which are not seen are eternal" (2 Cor. 4:18 NASB). Trust me, the spirit realm is alive and active. Its activity does not depend on our belief in or lack of belief in its existence. It is real and buzzing with activity 24 hours a day, 7 days a week. The spirit realm is never on vacation. God is always about the business of His Kingdom. And His business is ruling the entire universe for an eternity. I agree with the following quote from my friend Eddie Smith: "God is not waiting to rule. He is ruling now. As He listens to the prayers of His people, He continuously decrees and implements His purposes from the throne. The throne of God literally vibrates with divine activity."[1] Therefore, for us to be effective sons and daughters in His Kingdom we must not ignore the most active part of His creation. Why? Because as Scripture tells us concerning our position, we are seated with Him in heavenly places (see Eph. 2:6). If God is concerned about the spirit realm and He resides in the eternal spirit realm and our position is one of being seated with Him in heavenly places, then it is our responsibility to accept the reality of this vital portion of His Kingdom.

You might be asking, "But how do we know the spirit realm exists if we cannot fully see it?" I do not see electricity, but I know that it is real. I do not have understanding of how the words that I type in an email can travel over the Internet to another nation and appear as it was typed from my office over 1,000 miles away. Yet those words travel through cyberspace and appear. Truthfully, just because something might not be visible to the natural eye does not mean it doesn't exist. One of my favorite Scriptures of the many that reference this truth of the reality of the spirit realm is 2 Kings 6:15-17:

> *The servant of the man of God got up early and went out, and behold, there was an army with horses and chariots encircling the city. Elisha's servant said to him, "Oh no, my master! What are we to do?" Elisha answered, "Do not be afraid, for those who are with us are more than those who are with them." Then Elisha prayed and said, "Lord, please, open his eyes that he may see." And the Lord opened the servants eyes and he saw; and behold, the mountain was full of horses and chariots of fire surrounding Elisha* (AMP).

What an amazing supernatural encounter. However, this is where many in spiritual warfare sometimes get out of balance. They begin to believe that the enemy's army is always more powerful than God's army. I will reiterate. The enemy's army is real. There is a battle that has been raging for thousands of years. But no matter how hard satan tries, he will never change his doomed fate nor win the battle he is raging in the nations.

He has already lost. Some people focus on darkness to such an extent that they lose the ability to see that God is mighty, victorious, and able. And when we are in the assignments He has given to us, trust me, He ensures that there are more for us than against us. Those who get their focus out of balance, embrace fear, and shift their belief to promote darkness greater than light will receive the exact outcome they have placed their fear and faith in. Friends, hear me—where we place our expectancy there also will be the focus of our faith. Faith in the goodness and victory of God creates in us a victorious warfare stance. Faith aimed in the wrong direction will attract demonic attack. So am I stating that we will not experience warfare? Absolutely not. As believers we will. But how we respond is so very key. Do not allow the enemy to shift your place of faith nor rob your praise, worship, and thanksgiving to our heavenly Father.

But on the brighter side, the beauty of this story is that the spiritual reality of God's army became real to Elisha's servant. Elisha already had the spiritual sight and wisdom to know. His faith did not need to be adjusted. But when his servant's spiritual eyes were opened to understand, his fears of loss vanished. While some of us might not have the experience of seeing in the supernatural realm, obtaining understanding of this Kingdom truth at the beginning of this teaching is imperative. You will not hear in this book or this teaching that the enemy is more powerful than our God, but we will learn how to maneuver in that battle to be victorious. Why is it necessary to learn victorious warfare tactics? Underestimating the reality of the supernatural realm and spiritual battles is not a position of victory. Satan is a strategist, and he and his dark army are continuously implementing their schemes to kill, steal, and destroy. The truth is the battle is real.

Another imperative rule of warfare to begin to understand is that we cannot and must not be presumptuous in spiritual warfare. Clearly, Elisha was assigned to this battle. Therefore, the Lord sent the chariots and horses and the strategy for victory. Ignorance is never bliss when engaging in a battle. Elisha was not ignorant. God absolutely wants us to understand the wiles of the enemy and to be victorious in battle. However, we are not to come against everything we see or discern. We will discuss this further in Chapter Five, but I will briefly state here that the battles we are to fight are those the Lord has assigned to us and entrusted us with. Seeing my zealousness and feistiness, Peter Wagner many times gently reminded me, "Choose your battles wisely, darlin'. Only fight the battles the Lord is calling you to fight."

IS SPIRITUAL WARFARE IN THE WORD OF GOD?

The answer is yes! We know that the invisible realm is real and warfare occurs in the spirit realm because the principles appear throughout the Word of God. You may know and are very familiar with the words of Paul in Ephesians 6:12, "For our struggle is not against flesh and blood [contending only with physical opponents], but against the rulers, against the powers, against the world forces of this [present] darkness, against the spiritual forces of wickedness in the heavenly (supernatural) places" (AMP).

Sooner or later each believer discovers that the Christian life is and can be a battleground. It is not always a playground. We face an enemy we cannot defeat in our own strength. But with our Lord and the anointing of the Holy Spirit and strategies birthed in His glorious presence we are able to triumph. As we read further in Ephesians 6, we see Paul using the army to illustrate the believer's warfare with satan. While writing this passage, he himself was chained to a Roman soldier, and his readers were familiar with soldiers and the equipment they used. In fact, military illustrations seemed to be a favorite with Paul. I believe it is because he fully understood better than most the reality of spiritual warfare and how real the battle can be at times.

As Christians, we face three enemies—the world, the flesh, and the devil (see Eph. 2:1-3). The world refers to the systems and structures around us that are opposed to God. The flesh is the old nature that we inherited from Adam, a nature that is opposed to God and can do nothing spiritual to please God. And then of course there is satan and his army of darkness. But we know that by Jesus' death and resurrection, He overcame the world, the flesh, and the devil (see Eph. 1:19-23). Therefore, I want to help you hear the truth of my next statement. Allow the following understanding to begin to come alive in your Kingdom spiritual identity that as believers we do not fight *for* victory—we fight *from* victory! The Holy Spirit enables us, by faith, to appropriate Christ's victory for ourselves. When we receive salvation and are transformed into that new creation, His victory becomes our victory. And we are now positioned to appropriate that victory for ourselves. Let's investigate further examples from Scripture where we see victory realized.

Jesus Silencing an Unclean Spirit

The following is an example of what I will term *personal deliverance ministry*, sometimes referred to as casting out demons. Soon after beginning His earthly ministry, Jesus demonstrated that driving out evil spirits was a natural part of His mandate to set the oppressed free.

> *They went into Capernaum, and immediately on the Sabbath Jesus went into the synagogue and began to teach. They were completely amazed at His teaching; because He was teaching them as one having [God-given] authority, and not as the scribes. Just then there was a man in their synagogue with an unclean spirit; and he cried out [terribly from the depths of his throat], saying, "What business do You have with us, Jesus of Nazareth? Have You come to destroy us? I know who You are—the Holy One of God!" Jesus rebuked him, saying, "Be quiet (muzzled, silenced), and come out of him!" The unclean spirit threw the man into convulsions, and screeching with a loud voice, came out of him. They were all so amazed that they debated and questioned each other, saying, "What is*

this? A new teaching with authority! He commands even the unclean spirits (demons), and they obey Him" (Mark 1:21-27 AMP).

In Jesus' day, instructing in the synagogue usually involved thorough examination of the Scriptures given by a rabbi. Jesus taught in an unexpected way. It's likely that He was sitting and instructing out of His Kingdom wisdom and understanding for an extended time while the people listened, amazed, to His anointed words. The Scripture doesn't give us the exact subject of this particular teaching; however, I trust it concentrated on His focal message while on earth—*the Kingdom of God is near.* Meaning, "The Kingdom is within reach. It is directly before you. You can reach out and touch Me, understand, and receive revelation of who I am."

Hearing Jesus, this demonic spirit—unable to bear the pure, authoritative word from the Son of Man—manifested itself. First, the demon speaking through his human host asked, "What have You to do with us? Have you come to destroy us?" This demon was not referring to itself and the man through whom it spoke; it was voicing concern over the threat that Jesus' presence and teaching posed for the demonic realm. In other words, this demon was issuing a challenge from the entire demonic army: "This is *our* kingdom, not Yours!"

The demon then further exclaims, "I know who You are—the Holy One of God!" This might seem like an act of reverence, but the exact opposite is true. This unclean spirit was attempting to gain influence over our Lord by using His name and exposing His true identity. In ancient times, names were considered to represent the very essence of an individual. To know a person by name—his or her essence—and to announce their identity publicly was to have power over that person. This declaration was prompted by evil intent. The demon was trying to undermine the authority of the Savior of the world.

Jesus understood the evil plot behind this outburst and spoke immediately in the power of His authority. Most Bible translations interpret this rebuke as, *Be quiet!* To be honest, this is too nice. The more accurate translation of what Jesus verbalized is, *Shut up!*

There is an aspect of this confrontation that I want to emphasize. Notice that the defiant, rebellious spirit left, but it did so with a shriek. It is very probable that if a demon made a final show of rebellion against the Lord in a deliverance setting, the same outburst might occur when we issue commands in a deliverance setting.

WOMAN SET FREE FROM OCCULT DEDICATION

Hearing stories from the Bible greatly stirs our faith, but also hearing testimonies of current breakthrough stirs our faith even more. It causes the Word to come alive, and we clearly understand the same experiences that Jesus and the apostles encountered we too are to encounter and even more. My husband, Greg, and I have been involved in deliverance ministry since 1991. There are many testimonies we can share of great victory. Trust me when I say that God wants His children set free from strongholds.

I was ministering in Indonesia. The purpose of the trip was to help train and develop deliverance team members in the church we were partnering with. One foundational aspect I appreciate about this church is that they are building their membership from people newly saved. Once they receive salvation they are taken through an "Experiencing Freedom" weekend where they receive deliverance, and then they are placed into a mentoring program that equips them to become Kingdom influencers.

To facilitate this deliverance training, the pastor set up deliverance sessions with those needing freedom. The new team members served during the ministry sessions. Myself and Pam Ramirez, a powerful deliverance minister and woman of God, would rotate between the team sessions to mentor the new leaders. Allow me to say this. The type of encounter I am about to share is not the norm. Do dramatic encounters occur in times of ministry? The answer is yes, sometimes they do. I am using this session as an example to show that sometimes when we minister there can and will be encounters we will face even like those that Jesus faced.

After two days of ministry, Pam and I were enjoying a brief 15-minute break. Suddenly, we heard a loud demonic scream come from one of the rooms. We quickly made our way to the chaotic scene. Upon arriving, the team members were backed up against the wall not certain of what they were witnessing and baffled as how to handle it. Our attention was quickly drawn to the floor. The woman they were ministering to was slightly levitating above the floor while pulling herself around the room with the tips of her fingers. Her face was contorted, as she growled like a tiger.

I absolutely love my friend Pam. She always stays in a place of child-like faith, brings humor into almost every situation, but knows the authority and goodness of our Father. Calmly and quietly, we observed the situation. In a whisper Pam asked me, "Have you seen this before?"

I quietly replied, "No, this, I can say, I have not seen."

Upon hearing my voice, that demon went into a volatile manifestation. In a humanly impossible way, this woman's body instantly went from levitating to an upright standing position. She was inches from my face. The demon shrieked through her in its dark voice, "I hate you!"

Without missing a beat, Pam quipped a calm yet authoritative reply to that demon: "Oh, wrong thing to say to the prophet!" With Pam's response I could not help but laugh out loud, and I immediately commanded that spirit of witchcraft to leave the woman. She was radically set free that day and was so very grateful! We learned she was raised in a home of non-believers who were involved in occult witchcraft practices. One of the gods worshiped in this ancient demonic structure was a tiger god. In her childhood she had been dedicated to that entity.

To review, we were not looking for this dramatic encounter. We certainly did not provoke it. Nor was the demon's response to the sound of my voice one we were anticipating. The point of the story is, there is a demonic realm that is alive and active. There is such a thing as spiritual warfare.

Jesus' blood defeated satan and his army of darkness. When that authority is appropriated we can and will see people set free. And the beautiful truth is Jesus *wants* to see captives set free. He paid a high price to ensure freedom from the demonic realm. He gave His life on the cross as the sacrificial lamb and rose in resurrection life as the Lion of Judah who roars!

JESUS ENGAGED IN STRATEGIC WARFARE

Let's look at the events of Jesus' life leading up to the just-mentioned encounter with the unclean spirit. Following Jesus' baptism, He was led by the Spirit into the wilderness for forty days to be tempted by satan. Many might look at this as a defensive act, but actually this is not the case. Instead of going about His business and allowing satan to choose when he would attack Jesus, being led by the Spirit, took the offensive stance immediately following His baptism to put Himself in the position to overcome and gain victory. Interestingly, he was attacked by the enemy just as Adam and Eve were attacked—at their point of obedience to God.

> Before he announced His agenda in the synagogue of Nazareth, before he called the 12 disciples, before He preached the Sermon on the Mount, before He fed 5,000 or raised Lazarus from the dead, he knew He must engage in some crucial strategic-level spiritual warfare. The place Jesus chose is significant. He went to the "wilderness," which was known as a territory of satan. *The Dictionary of New Testament Theology* says of eremos, the Greek word for wilderness or desert, that it is "a place of deadly danger...and of demonic powers." If Jesus' encounter with the devil was to be decisive, the enemy should be given to use an athletic, "home field advantage." Jesus moved in on the devil's turf without hesitation and without fear.

Satan knew what the stakes were, and he gave it his best shot. He went so far as to offer Jesus his most priceless possession, "all the kingdoms of the world and their glory" (Matt 4:8). It was a crucial and ferocious battle, but the outcome was never in doubt. Satan's power never has been nor ever will be a match for the power of God. Jesus won. Satan was defeated. The power encounter cleared the way spiritually for all that Jesus was to accomplish over the next three years, including His death and resurrection.[2]

Do you see the pattern? After Jesus' baptism and His Father's recognition of His calling and destiny, a spiritual confrontation between satan and Jesus took place. What does this mean for us? As we enter into God-ordained destinies, we can be sure that we, too, will face seasons when the schemes of darkness come against us and our ministries. Being saved does not mean freedom from temptation; it means being equipped for victory over it.[3] Jesus had to stand and overcome the temptations of satan in the wilderness; we also will have times requiring a righteous stand. It is in these seasons that our blood-bought authority is tested and our faith and dependence on the Lord is stretched and strengthened. This results in tremendous, transforming spiritual growth. We will learn throughout our study that we overcome by the authority of Jesus' mighty name; the power of His shed blood; standing on the authoritative Word of God; and a pure, devoted, focused heart surrendered to Him in His glory.

CONTENDING AGAINST THE SPIRITS BEHIND ABORTION AND OVERCOMING A DEMONIC VISITATION

Because of my calling to deliverance, prophetic intercession, and strategic warfare prayer, there have been several instances when demonic entities have attempted to intimidate me from advancing. In one such occasion, we were contending against the spirits behind abortion.

My first trip into the state of Kansas was in 2005. I was invited to teach a group of hungry and attentive intercessors, pastors, and leaders. To my delight, it was observable that the Lord had placed me with a passionate army of believers who were prepared to begin this journey of spiritual mapping, welcoming prophetic revelation from the throne room, and who were passionate about setting into action warfare strategies to see social transformation realized.

Wichita, Kansas, housed an abortion clinic run by a doctor who was viewed by the public and self-satisfied as America's most productive abortionist, Dr. George Tiller. In his lifetime work, he aborted no less than sixty thousand unborn infants. Abortions, including late-term abortions, were the only medical procedures he executed in his practice.

I returned in the fall of 2007, which proved to be a divinely appointed and orchestrated spiritual warfare assignment. For months, believers in the state had been aggressively researching and praying that the spiritual root or demonic principality behind the notorious abortion clinic would be exposed. In preparation for our coming prophetic act, we prayed, asking the Lord to disclose the stronghold. At that moment, the Lord remarkably brought back to my memory a dream I had in 1994 in which He revealed to me the demonic spiritual entity lilith. She is cited in Isaiah 34:14 as the night monster. The Hebrew word is *lilim* or *lilith*, whose name means the night monster, night hag, or screeching owl (Strong's #H3917). In the dream the Lord expressly showed me this territorial deity to be one of the principal forces behind death and abortion. After further research, I understood why.

Lilith is an ancient deity that came from Babylonian and Assyrian mythology, but was also identified in later Jewish legends as a demon. She is also known as a woman who in rabbinic legend is Adam's first wife. She is supplanted by Eve and then becomes a demonic spirit. In this legend it is stated that she refused to lie submissively beneath Adam. She fled to the Red Sea. In occult witchcraft and mystic beliefs, it is said she gives birth daily to more than one hundred demons. She is depicted as a nocturnal great-winged goddess with bird-clawed feet. She carries a ring or rod of power, signifying that she is among the first-ranked gods. She is a seductress, replete with destruction, known as the goddess of death or Hades. I find this portion of her description interesting. In the dream in which the Lord allowed me to see her, she appeared just as described above. A seductress with a ring of power full of destruction and death. In occult witchcraft circles, they believe this dark entity has charge over all newborn infants, and she is worshiped with this understanding. While some might find this a little uncomfortable to discuss, this is a clear example of the reality of the spirit realm. When lucifer rebelled, he took a third of the angels with him. These angels are now functioning as dark angels and are part of satan's army. Lilith is one such dark angel who functions at the level of a principality. And when her name is referenced in Isaiah 34:14 she is being identified as such.

As I shared this revelation, we all believed this was the principality perpetuating death through abortion. The next day we drove to the airport for my return flight home. We decided to stop in front of the clinic to pray. As we prayed, I heard the voice of the Lord: "Becca, bind the territorial spirit operating behind the killings of this clinic." At the exact same time, the others in the car heard the Lord speaking this as well. I declared, "In the name of Jesus I bind the territorial spirit of death. I bind you, lilith, and say you no longer will be able to execute bloodshed of the innocent and unborn from this location!"

After my flight departed, a fierce windstorm blew across the state. Two days later, Sandy, the pastor, and her staff returned to the church offices only to come upon an amazing surprise. In the only tree on the church property an owl was bound with fishing line used to hang decorations. They called a wildlife ranger to the church to free it. The key point to remember is lilith is characterized as the screeching owl in the Bible!

Upon freeing the owl and examining it, the ranger said, "Based on the level of dehydration and the amount of bird waste below the tree, I can estimate how long the owl has been bound. Do you recall the windstorm that blew across the state two days ago? I believe the wind made it impossible for the owl to fly and forcefully blew it into the tree where the fishing line bound it."

Sandy called me and exclaimed, "Becca, one hour after you prayed and bound lilith, who is the screeching owl demonic entity of death, the Lord sent a sign. Through the windstorm, an owl was blown into our tree and bound by fishing line!" We both rejoiced and then prayed to receive the next piece of the prayer strategy.

For the next twenty-one days, at the leading of Chuck Pierce, believers across the nation began a period of fasting and prayer in the night hours. The idea behind this was to intercede and war when the demonic activity of lilith is the strongest in order to counter and defeat her strategies. It was an amazing twenty-one-day focus. During this time, I was leaving the prayer time in the early hours of the morning. As I entered my car to drive home, a demonic entity revealed itself in an attempt to intimidate me from moving forward in the assignment the Lord had entrusted to us. It fiercely stated, "If you continue in this assignment, you and your family will die." Understanding that this demon was coming against me because of what we were doing and the victory we were gaining, I was not intimidated. Instead, a righteous anger rose up from within me and I quickly bound it and began to joyfully sing out loud songs about the blood of Jesus. Needless to say, that proved to be a torment to that dark angel. Soon, I commanded it to leave, and it has never visited or harassed me again.

As the prayer focus continued, new legal cases were instituted against Dr. Tiller and his practice on top of the already existing ones. They focused on his repeated pattern of illegal late-term abortions.

"Tiller now faces two Board of Healing Arts investigations that could cost him his license. He faces 19 criminal counts of illegal late-term abortions that could cost him huge fines, and he faces a grand jury investigation that could net literally hundreds of additional counts of illegal abortions from the past five years that could cost him his freedom," said Operation Rescue president Troy Newman.[4]

Even patients began to come forward and give shocking revelations of all the illegal reasons given and actions surrounding their abortions.

From 2007 on, things continually intensified for Dr. Tiller. He was perpetually involved in court hearings and repeated accounts of his illegal activities within his medical practices were being exposed. Statistics show that the rate of post-viability abortions performed at Tiller's clinic dropped 23 percent in 2007 and the following years. Unfortunately, on May 31, 2009, Dr. George Tiller was tragically murdered. I need to state that Tiller's untimely death shocked and appalled all of us who were dealing with the sanctity of life in Kansas. It is a sad fact that he died after our spiritual warfare initiative, but this was not my desire nor the desire of anyone else on our team. Our prayers were focused on a much more benign closure to the high-profile advocacy of abortion in Kansas. However, following his untimely death, that abortion clinic was closed and the holocaust of babies at that clinic in Wichita ended.

GIDEON: SAVING A NATION

Over and over again we see in the Word of God the perpetuated cycle of sin, bondage, oppression, turning back to the Lord, and deliverance. One example is when the children of Israel turned away yet again and resumed their wickedness. God then "gave them into the hands of the Midianites" (Judg. 6:1 NIV). Year after year these fierce marauders pillaged Israel's vineyards and fields, and year after year the Israelites cowered in terror. The cries of the people were directed to heaven and the Lord heard:

Midian so impoverished the Israelites that they cried out to the Lord for help. When the Israelites cried out to the Lord because of Midian, he sent them a prophet, who said, "This is what the Lord, the God of Israel, says: I brought you up out of Egypt, out of the land of slavery. I rescued you from the hand of the Egyptians. And I delivered you from the hand of all your oppressors; I drove them out before you and gave you their land. I said to you, 'I am the Lord your God; do not worship the gods of the Amorites, in whose land you live.' But you have not listened to me" (Judges 6:6-10 NIV).

Gideon, a common young man who was consecrated to the Lord, was selected as the people's deliverer after the prophet revealed the Lord's response. While he was in the field threshing the wheat, minding his own business, an angel of the Lord appeared to him and said, "The Lord is with you, mighty warrior" (Judg. 6:12). Paraphrasing his response, Gideon said, "Who, me, Lord? I am the youngest and the weakest! How can I be the deliverer?"

The angel accepted no excuses and insisted that Gideon would be the leader to prevail against the oppressors and lead the people into battle to achieve a victory. While he was the leader, the land enjoyed peace for forty years (see Judg. 8:28), and Israel learned new yet timeless battle strategies.

KLAUS

The Lord spoke to us in 2017 to initiate an assignment in Ingolstadt, Bavaria. We had spent many hours in intercession and research to hear the Lord on how to advance in this strategic assignment of praying for this city, which through the occult practices of Adam Weishaupt had at one time negatively impacted Bavaria, Germany, and birthed and empowered demonic cultural ideologies throughout the world. Weishaupt's secret society of 3,000 members began to initiate plans to use their wealth to exert control within the cultures in which they lived and carried influence. (To read a thorough and historically accurate article about Adam Weishaupt and this group's lingering influence on world cultures today, I suggest "Meet the Man Who Started the Illuminati" by Isabel Hernandez. It can be found on the online *National Geographic* magazine.[5])

God did what I will term a "Jehovah sneaky moment." We decided to join a history tour led by the top historian of the city. We spent four hours with this expert as we walked through the streets. We ended in a cathedral in which a man by the name of Johann Eck is buried. In our previous research, we had not discovered anything about this man. On the tour, we quickly learned he was the main leader who spoke against and countered the reformation movement birthed through Martin Luther. Not only did he totally disagree with the Protestant Reformation, he was one of the key spiritual leaders of that time who wanted all activity and power of the Holy Spirit removed from the church. He perpetuated the belief that the Holy Spirit was only to be depicted by a picture of a dove descending on Jesus, removing the reality that He is a person with a personality. Friends, God is amazing in how He sets up our paths. We were in this city on a prayer assignment on the 500-year anniversary of the Reformation. Now in an unplanned divine moment, we were literally standing on top of Johann Eck's grave (he was buried in the floor of the cathedral).

The next day, which happened to be Pentecost, we returned, sat ourselves in the alcove dedicated to Johann Eck, and began to pray. We repented for the stance against the Reformation, repented for the removal of the Holy Spirit from the Church. We broke a spirit of religion, death, violence, and witchcraft as we had learned that heavy fighting and killing had occurred between the Protestants and Catholics. There was a history of tremendous bloodshed. We asked the Lord to bring His healing touch. As we prayed, we felt the Lord leading us to worship. We went to our knees in that alcove positioned above the grave of this dead man and began to worship the Lord as a group out loud. As we exalted the Lord, the cathedral went quiet and the Lord's glory fell in that place. Tangible glory. It was powerful beyond words.

In obedience to the Lord's leading, we made our way to the next location, which was the original oratorio or study hall of Ingolstadt University where Adam Weishaupt had spent many hours deep in study as a student and a professor, along with the leaders of his secret society. This is the school that greatly taught on the removal of the Holy Spirit. It is also a location of focused idol worship toward several forms of a demonic entity by the name of the queen of heaven. One icon carries the name minerva, queen of wisdom and the other maria de victoria. At the front of the hall was an altar, and positioned directly in front of it was a stage for music and theatrical performances. The caretaker happily greeted us, introducing himself as Klaus. We quickly realized he spoke little English. Making our way to the front of the hall, I noticed a sign advertising a classical voice recital scheduled for that weekend. I explained to Klaus that I am a classically trained vocalist and inquired if I could sing on the stage in order to experience the beautiful acoustics. This is something I have initiated numerous times. Surprisingly, God's glory falls each time and miracles begin to happen.

I sang two lines of a German aria. To add a note on the greatness of God and His ability to work through us supernaturally, I have not trained classically for over 28 years. If the vocal chords are not correctly and consistently exercised, the pure operatic voice is lost. However, I have not lost the purity of my trained operatic sound. This is miraculous.

Klaus loved the aria and asked me to sing again. I gladly obliged by singing "Amazing Grace." The Holy Spirit moved mightily. It had been cold in that hall, but suddenly it grew hot. Klaus was sweating profusely, wiping his brow while laughing in joy. The fire and glory enveloped him. Overcome with joy, one of the team members suggested that we all sing. Now it is important to convey that not everyone on that team could carry a tune. They gathered around me, and I jokingly whispered, "You guys better sing good!"

We all began to worship. To the team's surprise, it was glorious. Klaus could barely contain himself as the glory literally washed over him. Joyously we explained to him it was Jesus and the Holy Spirit. He excitedly exclaimed in broken English, "Yes! Jesus is nice! Jesus is good! Jesus is wonderful!" He then shared, "Some other churches come here. They not so hot. You are hot!" (He was referring to the fire of God's presence in that room that was now resting on him.) While he continued to laugh and perspire under the anointing of God, he put his finger on the pulse of his wrist and exclaimed, "My heart race so fast! Jesus nice! Jesus good! Jesus wonderful!"

What joy it brings to relive this testimony. When we choose to allow God to use us, awesome things can transpire. On Pentecost Day on the 500-year anniversary of the Reformation, the Holy Spirit, through the sound of praise and worship, suddenly invaded the place where His very presence had been shunned and mocked. It was the miracle moment and day of Klaus' salvation and Holy Spirit baptism. The name *Klaus* means "the people's victory." This prophetic moment was a first-fruits sign and wonder of the promises that are ahead for the beautiful people of this city and for the nation of Germany.

GETTING RID OF
THE HINDRANCES

No man is greater than his prayer life. The pastor
who is not praying is playing; the people who are not
praying are straying. ...We have many organizers, but
few agonizers; many players and payers, few pray-ers;
many singers, few clingers; lots of pastors, few wrestlers;
many fears, few tears; much fashion, little passion;
many interferers, few intercessors; many writers, but
few fighters. Failing here, we fail everywhere.
—LEONARD RAVENHILL, *Why Revival Tarries*

After reading the first two chapters, you might be experiencing a stirring,
wanting to draw closer to the Lord, and also an awakening to function in
Kingdom authority. The following is a prayer to invite Him into this process as we continue through this teaching.

Lord, I desire to have a deeper relationship with You. I desire more of You, to have encounters with You in the Holy of Holies, the glory realm. It is my heart's desire to see revival. Lord, to be one who partners with You in bringing transformation. Lord, cause me to be one who walks effectively in the spiritual authority that You have given me. One to birth strategies to see Your Kingdom come and that cause demons and darkness to flee. Lord, as I read the pages of this book I welcome You into the process to teach me how!

In order to advance into the abiding place and increased authority, it is key to discover the hindrances that hold us back from experiencing the dimensions of increase available to all believers. Therefore, let's take the time in this chapter to identify those things that might be hindering the fullness of walking as ones anointed in His glory for victorious warfare.

THE DISTRACTION OF BUSYNESS

Intamacy

Trust me, once there is a commitment to consistent time with Him, the enemy will come and hinder this dedicated time. Our culture keeps us way too busy and consistently pulled in multiple directions. What is viewed as an overly busy schedule full of distractions or the demands of others might actually be the enemy at work to keep us out of the Lord's presence. Or maybe the issue struggled with is the inability to say no when boundaries need to be established to protect our time with Him. Jesus gently corrected Martha when she brought the complaint against Mary concerning her choice to sit at the feet of Jesus. The Becca Greenwood paraphrase of the Bible says, "Lord, there is much to be done. Look how busy I am, but she is choosing to sit at Your feet." His response: "Martha, you are worried over many things. But Mary has chosen the best—that which will remain." I realize we all get pulled in many directions in our hurried world. And there is much to accomplish for Him and His Kingdom. But we must be consistent in dedicated time with the Lord. As Leonard Ravenhill so aptly stated, "No man is greater than his prayer life." It is in this no-distraction zone with Him that we are anointed, empowered to maneuver through all those Kingdom assignments the Holy Spirit is speaking to us to fulfill. He is our lifeline. He expands our spiritual capacity of power to awakening and understanding of the authority we rightfully have inherited to engage.

break spirts
hindering, delaying, Obstructing

SPIRIT OF DELAY

Or perhaps a spirit of delay is holding back the promises of the Lord. What is a spirit of delay? It is a spirit that is unleashed to keep us out of God's time. It will bring circumstances, distractions. It will hinder, put off to a later time, postpone. It will impede the process of moving forward and advancing. As a result, weariness and feelings of being overwhelmed will begin to take hold in order to rob strength or the desire to move forward. If these demonic schemes succeed, then unbelief takes hold. Lies will begin to invade our thoughts and emotions. For example: "His promises will not come to pass. God cannot use you. He is not for you."

The truth is, everything in this earth is not in submission to the Lord as of yet. We must allow the warrior within us to rise up and bring correction to that which has not aligned with God and His purposes. When the enemy and his army of darkness are delaying our Kingdom promises, we must speak out loud and demand these evil spirits to stop. We recently hosted a conference in 2017 titled Engage. My dear friend and mentor in my life, Cindy Jacobs, was a keynote speaker and released an anointed prophetic message on the spirit of delay. She emphatically decreed out loud in a warfare stance over the corporate group, "*Basta!*" (The Spanish word for *enough!*) Hear me, if delay is coming against you, there must be a warrior's cry that rises up and that decrees, "Basta! Enough!" When a demonic force is at play and holding back destiny and promises, begging God is not going to bring the breakthrough. We must break those demonic assignments and bind all schemes of the enemy that are hindering, delaying, and obstructing.

The Lord Dealing with Delay in My Life

Or maybe the delay you are experiencing is by your own choosing, as was the personal choice and challenge I faced many years ago. Allow me to explain. The year was 1992. My friend had purchased the book *Rees Howells, Intercessor* for me as a gift. I noticed that every morning when reading a chapter in the book, the previous night I had dreamt what was unfolding in the pages of the book. Only in many of the dreams, I discovered it was me having the experiences that I would read in the book concerning Rees Howells and his journey in the calling as an intercessor. It was evident the Lord was speaking, but I was uncertain of the fullness of what was transpiring.

One night I had a very vivid dream. Our oldest daughter, Kendall, was two. She was sitting on a pier, feet dangling off the edge, gazing down on the refreshing body of water below. I was watching her from the top of a hill and intuitively knew she was going to jump into that deep pond. I began shouting to two pregnant women who were supposed to be watching her, but my cries of alarm went unheard. I was deeply concerned because I knew she would not be able to keep herself afloat. I began to run down the hill toward the pier, shouting, "Kendall, baby, don't jump!" But the temptation of the cool water proved too strong and eagerly she pushed herself off that pier.

Oftentimes the Lord will speak to us in a dream language that will be familiar. In my teenage years, I had worked as a lifeguard and swim instructor, so the scene in this dream would definitely strike a chord of understanding. I rushed to the edge of the pier and without hesitation dove in after Kendall. My baby was sinking under that deep muddy water. But instead of being panicked, she locked eyes with mine. I noticed a distinct bright light, like the glory of the Lord, shining across her face. Even though she was sinking, Kendall was in total peace.

Because I had run so quickly, I was completely out of breath. One key that you learn in life saving is you can't save someone if you yourself are drowning. No longer able to hold my breath, I quickly swam to the surface, gulped in a deep breath of air, and pulled myself under water to rescue my baby. It was the same scene as before. She was sinking with her hand outstretched toward mine, yet still at total peace. As the tips of my fingers touched hers, she suddenly slipped out of view, into the depths of the muddy water. This so startled me that I woke myself out of the dream, rushed into her room, and swept her up out of her bed into my arms and began to weep while rocking her back and forth.

This dream was beyond real to me. I felt I had lived it. For three days I ignored the Lord every time He nudged me to pick up the book and finish reading it. Finally, at the encouragement of my friend that this book and the life of Rees Howells had something to do with my calling of intercession to the nations, I decided to continue reading. I was nervous and questioned the Lord, "Lord, are You going to tell me I have to give up my daughter? Am I about to lose her?" As I read the next chapter, I was not encouraged. I discovered that Rees and his wife, Elizabeth, were called to Africa to birth revival. They had a precious baby boy, Samuel. He was eight months old. The area in Africa in which they would engage in mission work was too dangerous for a baby. Therefore, they gave Samuel to Rees' uncle and aunt to raise during the ten-year period of living abroad. Now I was really disturbed. I sat in my prayer closet and wept. "Lord, why did You give me this dream? Am I going to have to give up my child to go to the nations?"

The Lord spoke very clearly to me, "Becca, I am calling you to the nations. Where I have called you, I have called your family. You will have more children. But I am asking you to lay Greg, Kendall, and your future children on the altar and give them to Me."

My first thought was, "Here am I, Lord, send Greg!" My second thought was, "What will people think? I am a woman. Everyone will label me as a bad mother. Lord, can I wait until Kendall and my future children are eighteen?"

The Lord gently spoke, "Yes, you can. But obedience is better than sacrifice. If you will step in and begin to move toward your calling now, it will provide a righteous inheritance for your children and the generations to come. It will produce a hunger in them for the nations. Don't you know I love Kendall and your future children even more than you do? I can take better care of them than you while you are in the nations. My grace is sufficient. The choice is yours."

Weeping as I lay prostrate on the floor of my prayer closet, I laid Greg, Kendall, and my future children at the feet of Jesus and said, "Here I am, Lord, use me."

And friends, the Lord has been faithful to His promise and the revelation He shared is unfolding in the spiritual lives of all three of our daughters. They all dearly love the Lord and have a heart to faithfully serve Him. Two work for our ministry and all three of them are involved in serving the Lord and traveling to nations with me.

Discernment
Waiting, listening,
hearing Him,

STRIVING TO PERFORM OR TO ATTAIN ACCEPTANCE

Oftentimes we feel or believe that striving will lift us to a position to enter into the glory. Striving keeps us in the soulish realm, in the flesh. We cannot build a relationship if all we are doing is talking about ourselves, making every conversation about ourselves and our needs, and never learning to listen or hear the other person we are relating to. The same is true in the Spirit. We must learn the art of waiting, listening, and hearing Him. This creates a depth in each of us that will cause the fruit of learning not to attack everything we see.

Discerning a demonic spirit is not an initial calling to instantly attack it or war against it. If I came against or "took on" every demon I heard or saw, I would be worn out. What do I mean? I have a strong gift of discernment and am able to discern and fairly consistently know the spiritual condition of those I am in proximity to. Being continuously around groups of people in airports, conferences, meetings, and seminars, it would be exhausting to address every stronghold or lie of the enemy I discern in the spirit. That would prove to be an open door of striving and exhaustion.

Many warriors tend to get into striving and battle everything they see. The enemy discerns those who have learned the art of waiting and listening to the Lord's voice. This is demonstrated by the demonic spirit who manifested at the failed deliverance session led by the seven sons of Sceva: "Jesus I know, and Paul I know; but who are you?" (Acts 19:15 NKJV). None of us want to hear from the enemy's camp that we are not known. How well you are known in heaven—yielded to His Spirit, His Word, His truth—will cause the Kingdom authority, given in fullness as an inheritance upon salvation, to increase and manifest in way that will hit the mark in the spirit and bring breakthrough. In this unfortunate spiritual encounter involving the seven sons of Sceva, the demons saw no evidence of a yielded life, the glory, or the sound of authority that comes from one who has spent time in the Holy of Holies, in beyond the veil encounters.

THE POWER OF SPOKEN WORDS

What we speak and say is important. James 1:26 says, "If anyone thinks himself to be religious, and yet does not bridle his tongue but deceives his own heart, this man's religion is worthless" (NASB). Many of us have heard others speak out negative confessions, gossip, and react emotionally in anger with harsh words that curse. And maybe some of us have done this ourselves. Or even cursed ourselves with our own spoken words. When God created the universe, He did so with His spoken Word. There is creative power in words. What you speak and profess out loud will begin to unfold. The truth is, you become your own prophet. The following passage from James 3:2-10 states it clearly:

For we all stumble in many ways. If anyone does not stumble in what he says, he is a perfect man, able to bridle the whole body as well. Now if we put the bits into the horses' mouths so that they will obey us, we direct their entire body as well. Look at the ships also, though they are so great and are driven by strong winds, are still directed by a very small rudder wherever the inclination of the pilot desires. So also the tongue is a small part of the body, and yet it boasts of great things.

See how great a forest is set aflame by such a small fire! And the tongue is a fire, the very world of iniquity; the tongue is set among our members as that which defiles the entire body, and sets on fire the course of our life, and is set on fire by hell. For every species of beasts and birds, of reptiles and creatures of the sea, is tamed and has been tamed by the human race. But no one can tame the tongue; it is a restless evil and full of deadly poison. With it we bless our Lord and Father, and with it we curse men, who have been made in the likeness of God; from the same mouth come both blessing and cursing. My brethren, these things ought not to be this way (NASB).

Do you hear this powerful truth? Your tongue is a fire. Interestingly enough, this word *fire* is the same word used in Acts 2 when tongues of fire were distributed on the 120 in the Upper Room. We can speak the fire of the flesh and enemy or we can speak the glory and fire of the Kingdom of God, His Word, and His truth. Just as negative words spoken out against ourselves or by others can burn up our walk, our words spoken out against others cause difficulty and warfare in their walks as well. It is our choice. Instead of speaking out negatively and releasing a curse, we can choose to speak the truth of Him, His Word, and His goodness. Bridling our tongue and guarding our words should become an intentional focus so we can become effective glory carriers and warriors.

Bridle our tongue

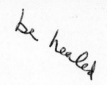

be healed

WOUNDED WARRIOR

There are many warriors in the Body of Christ who are wounded, who have a chink in their armor that needs to be mended. Allowing wounds to go unhealed prevents us from entering into His glory. And as a word of wisdom, entering into warfare while wounded is an open door for harassment and counterattack. Psalm 23:3 tells us, "He restores my soul." He wants our soul—our mind, will, and emotions—to be healed and whole. We all have experienced ungodly actions, untrue words, rejection, betrayal, and accusations spoken against or over us. And these words carry a weight in the spirit to pierce and wound. The enemy can and will use the words and/or actions of others whose genuine motive in their hearts is not intended to hurt you. Oftentimes, those who speak damaging words that obscure destiny might not even realize they are not speaking the truth. Without intending to, they partnered with the enemy and were speaking the enemy's intentions out loud. Woundedness in our soul causes inaccuracy in our hearing. If we have wounds, it is time to <u>be healed</u>.

Unoffendable

Are We Willing to Live a Lifestyle of Forgiveness?

The most difficult situations to overcome are the wounds by those who are intentionally wounding, especially those whom we have loved and established close relationship with. Here is where we have to choose to invite the Lord to lead us into a <u>lifestyle of forgiveness</u>. The enemy will use anyone or anything to disqualify our prayers. Our Father does recognize that we have been wronged; however, He still requires forgiveness. We cannot stay connected into or vitally united to what the Spirit of God is doing if we have <u>offenses</u> that <u>develop into bitterness</u>.

I was studying the Word and was led to the scene of Jesus praying in the Garden of Gethsemane. Can you imagine what that night must have been like for Jesus? He knew the suffering and agony He was about to endure. Really, it was an intensity that is beyond difficult to fathom. When the crowd arrived with Judas in the garden to arrest Him, Peter as always was his radical self. He drew a sword and cut off the ear of a servant of the high priest. Jesus instantly rebuked Peter, picked up the ear, and supernaturally healed that man. As I studied this, I heard the voice of Jesus, "Becca, I healed that man so he could play his part in ensuring the torturous beatings I endured and the crucifixion." I was silent at first and then emotionally undone. If Jesus can forgive for all the betrayals, wounds, and the horrible suffering on that cross—and heal a man in order that he could play his role in this process of condemning and persecuting Jesus—then friends, we too can forgive. When you are hooked into unforgiveness, you cannot be hooked into God's love, presence, throne room, or glory. There will be a wall of hindrance blocking your entrance. There will be no victory in warfare.

Key

Receive Healing from Wrong Judgments and Critical Words

The wrong judgments and resulting critical words of others do not determine your destiny and purpose. While they do cause pain, allow Him to touch those areas of hurt with His amazing, beautiful love and healing. It is the promises of God and your faithfulness and obedience to those promises and to Him that secure your path. Jesus was greatly criticized, but He forgave and stayed the course that His Father designed for Him. These moments in time are opportunities to become more like Him. Allow His character to be forged in you. Shake off the negative, critical words and judgments of others who try to place their incorrect expectations on you and do not embrace these words or actions as part of your identity. Absolutely choose to forgive or there will be a delay of moving into the new season. His supernatural, immeasurable love empowers you with the ability to forgive and removes the sting of the pain. Stay the course with Him. Keep your gaze on Him. He will never fail you. He is a faithful God.

A Lifestyle of Instant Repentance?

A directive that all believers must learn to intentionally step into is praying daily that the Lord will keep you from temptation and evil. Invite the Holy Spirit to bring conviction when you have sinned. When you feel that conviction, instantly repent. Don't allow the sun to go down on your anger and wrath.

> *The [reverent] fear and worshipful awe of the Lord includes the hatred of evil; pride and arrogance and the evil way, and the perverted mouth, I hate* (Proverbs 8:13 AMP).

Restitution and Reconciliation

> *So if you are presenting your offering at the altar, and while there you remember that your brother has something [such as a grievance or legitimate complaint] against you, leave your offering there at the altar and go. First make peace with your brother, and then come and present your offering* (Matthew 5:23-24 AMP).

When we approach God we must first be right with others. Some of us have broken relationships with others that need to be made right. The Lord makes it plain that we cannot have a good relationship with Him if we are not reconciling relationships with others. Broken relationships create a hole in our armor. Ask the Lord if there are broken relationships in your life. Make a list and begin to seek healing and restoration.

Oftentimes we think of a grievance or a complaint as actions or words. But have you made financial promises that have not been honored? Have you borrowed money and never repaid it? Some have a trail of unpaid bills and have resolved with intention to not pay that bill. This in turn can be a hindrance to walking in the glory and anointed for victory. Ask the Lord to show you any area where you need to make restitution and for the ability and the plan to do it.

*Fear God
not man (any man, or thing)*

WHOM DO YOU FEAR?

Fear can weave a web of doubt. Trust me when I say I know this to be true. I used to be bound by a spirit of fear but was radically set free twenty-eight years ago. Fear of man, heights, dark, phobias, anxiety, worry can immobilize us when we should take action. It acts as a gag order binding us into silence when we should speak. It feels powerful, but its power is deceptive. That's why the Bible tells us, "The fear of man lays a snare, but whoever trusts in the Lord is safe" (Prov. 29:25 ESV). The Hebrew word here for "snare" refers to traps hunters used to catch animals or birds. Snares are dangerous. If we get caught, we must do whatever it takes to free ourselves.

Each of us instinctively knows and understands that our existence fits into a larger purpose or story. Deep down, we know our purpose is connected to our heavenly Father. Why is this important to acknowledge? The person to whom we ascribe most authority—to define who we are, our worth, what we should do, and how we should do it—is the person we fear the most because it is the person whose approval we want most. You obey the one you fear. Does God want us fearful? The answer is no. Allow me to explain what I am saying.

God designed us in a way that reveals who and what our heart loves. This is why the Bible so often commands us to "fear the Lord."

> *And now, Israel, what does the Lord your God require of you, but to fear the Lord your God, to walk in all his ways, to love him, to serve the Lord your God with all your heart and with all your soul, and to keep the commandments and statutes of the Lord, which I am commanding you today for your good?* (Deuteronomy 10:12-13 ESV)

Trusting God is safe; fearing man is not. God usually teaches us this through the lesson of obeying in spite of our feelings. For then we learn to trust God's promises more than our perceptions and reach the place where we can assuredly say, "The Lord is my helper; I will not fear" (Heb. 13:6 ESV). God has the power to free us, and He wants us living in the safe freedom of trusting Him. He frees us by helping us face our false fears so that they lose their power over us. Allow me to share a powerful testimony.

Several years ago, I was involved in an international spiritual warfare assignment with intercessors from around the world. Several team members were praying on a high mountain. The remainder of the team members were interceding for their mission that night from a lower location. We had been in intercession for long hours and decided to take a short dinner break. As the food was brought to the table, suddenly I felt an alarm in my spirit and immediately jumped from the table and began to run to the prayer room shouting, "We must pray now!" All of the other team members instantly followed my lead. Arriving in the prayer room we began to intercede and war for the safety of the team climbing to the high place for the purpose of strategic intercession. Without knowledge in the natural, but in the Spirit, we knew that there was an avalanche heading toward them. We began to decree, "No weapon formed against this team shall prosper!" We prayed until the burden left.

A couple of hours passed, and the team radioed down. At the exact time we were interceding, there was indeed an avalanche barreling down the mountain toward the team. The leader, in anointed glory wisdom, shouted, "Turn your back to the avalanche!" and then decreed out loud, "Whom we fear the most and put our trust in, His glory will be our covering and shield!" Friends, miraculously, that avalanche barreled down the mountain a few hundred feet beyond them. However, as it approached the group in a deafening roar the avalanche parted and did not touch them.

Whom we fear the most, His glory will be our covering and shield. Fear has got to go! It is a magnet for spiritual attack, harassment, and backlash. Stop being afraid of what could go wrong and start being excited about what could go right.

Laziness Moves Us into Slumber

> *Laziness casts one into a deep sleep [unmindful of lost opportunity], and the idle person will suffer hunger* (Proverbs 19:15 AMP).

> *So that you will not be [spiritually] sluggish, but [will instead be] imitators of those who through faith [lean on God with absolute trust and confidence in Him and in His power] and by patient endurance [even when suffering] are [now] inheriting the promises* (Hebrews 6:12 AMP).

Laziness can cause us to go into a deep sleep. It numbs our spiritual senses, causes our spiritual eyes and ears to grow dull, and if practiced for too long it will rob us of inheriting the promises that our heavenly Father desires for us to experience in our spiritual lives, our walk, and in our prayers.

Shake off Regret

Don't continue to look at the failures of the past. Learn the necessary lessons in order to not repeat the patterns of the past. Some might be feeling the enemy trying to pull you back into old places and ways of thinking or trying to cause a stirring in your emotions that leads to discouragement that was experienced in an old season. Failures do not disqualify us. Do not get stuck in the wilderness of disappointment. Shake off the regret from the past season and begin to move forward. If you need an increase in faith, be with others who are operating in the faith you need. Their manifested faith to move beyond can become your faith to get you to the next season.

JESUS IS A LOVER AND A WARRIOR

Do you struggle with the belief that there really is such a thing as warfare? Or even more so, do you struggle with the concept that we need to know about warfare and engage in it? Is there a struggle in your mind that Jesus only loves and He is not a warrior? Allow me to share my personal testimony.

Because of our involvement in deliverance and strategic intercession, oftentimes I will get asked this question, "Are you a lover or a warrior?" The question is presented to me as if I would need to give an answer in a way that would place me in a certain category—one, but not the other. My answer has always been, "I am both." Everything we do in intercession, prophecy, deliverance, healing, and in strategic assignments is birthed from the place of intimacy with the Lord. We only do the assignments He speaks to us and entrusts to us in that place of intimacy, in His glory. Everything in our lives and our Christian walk should come from the place of His glorious presence and the truth of His Word. Because of the love and intimacy we have with Him, He then entrusts us with those assignments He has called us to. And, yes, even the warfare assignments we engage in.

I realize there are examples in the Body of Christ who engage in spiritual warfare but do not practice this foundational principle to be effective in assignments. I have been pondering and seeking the Lord for how to address the concept that to cause warfare to cease, our primary weapon is to love Jesus more. I absolutely do believe we are to love Jesus more in all areas of our lives, and without a doubt we are to love others with His heart. However, I will state this plainly. You cannot love a demon out of a person. You cannot love darkness, strongholds, principalities out of a region. You can and must absolutely love the people and the land and regions He is assigning you to. And absolutely, to gain an understanding of how to maneuver in the authority the Lord has given us, we die to ourselves and love Him more. Love, love, love Jesus and the people and the land with all your heart. But satan and demons do not flee just because of love. People respond to the love of Jesus, and when we encounter that love, it causes an authority to rise up in us to command demons to leave. We must learn to distinguish between the two and yet function in both.

If it were true that loving Jesus more is the main or only weapon in our arsenal that causes satan and demons to cease in their warfare tactics, then it seems to me that lucifer would have never rebelled against our heavenly Father. He and his dark army lived in perfect, holy, glorious love and chose to despise and rebel against it. Satan and his army of darkness hate that our heavenly Father loves us and that we love Him and one another. They want to separate us from this love. So we must determine in our hearts to be lovers of the Lord and not allow circumstances or warfare to rob us of this place of loving Him and others. While the demonic realm does recognize that we are lovers of Jesus, darkness flees when we resist. What the demonic realm does recognize is the power of the blood of Jesus, the truth of Jesus and His immeasurable authority that He reigns as King of kings and Lord of lords for eternity. The demonic realm does respond and flee when we speak forth the truth of His Word and we rise up in the authority He has given us and command darkness to go. One of the other key weapons of warfare is when we engage in abandoned praise and worship to our Father, released in Spirit and in truth. Satan and His army want to rob our worship and keep us bound from lifting our voices to glorify Him! We must never allow darkness to rob our praise to our King. Allow me to explain further by sharing a clear word the Lord recently spoke to me as I began to write this manuscript.

Greg and I were walking through the airport on our way to Scotland. I heard the Lord speak very clearly: "Becca, this message needs to be conveyed to the Church. The greatest lovers make the greatest warriors because they have a cause to fight from and to fight for." Friends, the truth is Jesus is a lover and a warrior. He is not either/or. He is both/and. When we encounter Him and His amazing love and magnificent glory, those things that He so passionately loves will begin to matter to us, and what He is passionate about and is fighting for we too will fight *for* along *with* Him. And what He is passionate about seeing defeated and broken in the demonic

2020
Courage & Passion
Cinnamon

realm we will also carry that same passion and burden. And that passion and burden in the abiding glory place will cause us to rise up and war.

When I encountered the Lord in a dramatic way in 1992, I knew He was fighting on behalf of me and for me in order that I would be free. There was no doubt that He was there to set me free. My place was to come into the realization at that moment that if Jesus gave His life for me, shed His blood for me, rose from the grave in resurrection life, He has already won that battle for me. Meaning, no matter what the enemy brought against me and tried to torment me with to keep me spiritually bound, when I repented and submitted myself to the Lord, His love and the blood He shed on the cross paved the way for me to be delivered and set free. When I saw and heard Jesus in this glory encounter of immense love and victorious authority, my spiritual eyes of understanding were opened. I was completely undone. I had been captured by His holy love and empowered through His endless authority. And in this moment it caused me to rise up in confidence. Weeping, I verbally proclaimed, "Jesus, I see You. And if You are here with me and fighting for me then I am going to get in the fight with You!" I was radically set free that night from guilt, shame, torment, and depression. When I saw Jesus in that encounter He was a great lover. He was also a great warrior. So awesome and holy—full of love. Surrounded by the wind and fire of the Holy Spirit. He was magnificent and spoke with the unshakable authority of the King of kings and the Lord of lords—the Savior of the world who rules and reigns for eternity!

To be honest with you, I loved at that moment and still love today the warrior Jesus. I don't want to experience only a portion of who He is; I desire to experience as many of His attributes that He allows me to experience. Love, joy, peace, comfort, majesty, holiness, power, authority!

In closing this testimony, I will share His word again: "The greatest lovers make the greatest warriors because they have a cause to fight from and to fight for." Jesus is the greatest lover and warrior of all time. And it is a privilege to love and war in the assignments He entrusts to us to see His

Kingdom extended, a harvest reaped, and an awakening of transformation. We war from the encounters in His glory to see breakthrough come.

STRATEGIES FOR
WARFARE REVEALED

The conqueror overcomes within the framework
of God's program of prayer and faith. The prayer
closet is the arena that produces the overcomer.
—PAUL BILHEIMER, *Destined for the Throne*

As we resolved, Jesus is a lover and a warrior. He was moved to compassion and He healed the sick. He was challenged by demons and cast them out. He was tempted by satan in the wilderness in an offensive move and overcame in victory. He wept at the tomb of Lazarus and then raised him from the dead. Colossians 2:15 states very clearly His triumph over darkness: "And having disarmed the powers and authorities, he made a public spectacle of them, triumphing over them by the cross" (NIV). Jesus brought trouble to, frightened, conquered, and established victory over satan and his kingdom of darkness when He made a public spectacle of them as He hung on that cross, three days later rose from the grave, and then ascended into heaven to sit at the right hand of our Father making a way for us to ascend to be more than conquerors and ones who are ready to war.

GLORY ENCOUNTERS THAT MARKED ME FOR DESTINY

I have been in that throne room with Jesus and our heavenly Father and encountered Him many times in my prayer room, in dreams and visions, and in corporate gatherings. The first encounter that I experienced with Him was life-altering and set the course for destiny.

It was 1991, and I and my husband, Greg, and our oldest daughter Kendall were moving to Houston and were there on a house-hunting trip. Alice Smith, a dear friend and mentor, was our real estate agent. She arranged for us to attend a Benny Hinn meeting that Friday evening before looking at homes the next day. We had recently read *Good Morning, Holy Spirit* and it greatly impacted our spiritual walk and created an awakened spiritual hunger. Our expectancy was high as this was the first time we would attend one of Benny's public gatherings.

We were seated in the nosebleed section in the middle of the auditorium. Thousands of people were present. The worship was beautiful, the presence of the Holy Spirit glorious. Benny's message stirred faith and an ushered in a true glory presence of the Lord. Throughout the service I became very aware of a deep yearning and passion that was being unlocked within me. As the service drew to an end, Benny felt the Lord leading him to do something that he normally did not do. He asked, "Who wants to experience more of the presence of the Holy Spirit? Who wants an encounter with Him, an impartation of the anointing? If that's you, put your hands up!" It felt that this invitation was released just for me. Without hesitation, I threw my hands up in the air. Instantly, I began to tremble. Alice asked, "Do you need healing?"

"No," I replied.

She confidently exclaimed, "Well, this is obviously the Lord, so we are going with it!"

The presence was so wonderful, I gladly exclaimed, "No arguments here!"

Immediately following our exchange. Benny raised his hand and shouted the words, "Take it, take it, take it!" thrusting his hand forward in unison with each decree he released. As soon as the first declaration of "Take it" was exclaimed, I suddenly flew backward in the air as if struck by a bolt of lightning. He shouted out the phrase again. Again, I was jolted while a surge of intense energy rushed through my body. One final time he declared, "Take it!" I was catapulted through the air, landing on the floor, slain in the Spirit. As a reminder, we were seated in the nosebleed section of a huge auditorium. This is not what I would term a courtesy fall. I was unaware until that evening that people could be slain in the Spirit.

Friends, I was totally gone, unaware of my earthly surroundings and in the throne room of heaven at the feet of Jesus and our heavenly Father. It was wonderful, holy, beyond human words. I began to weep, "Jesus, please, let me stay." I did not want to leave Him or His presence. He was everything my heart had ever desired. He so lovingly yet with great holiness spoke, "Becca, you must go back. You have a husband and a daughter. You will have more children. I brought you here to experience Me and My throne room. It is from here, from this moment, and from this place that you will begin to walk in your calling. From this anointing and glory presence in My throne room." I can still hear the power of His words and feel His magnificent presence as I type this. This initial encounter changed my life forever, and it is the driving force behind all that I do now in my walk with Him. It was the launching point of destiny that was spoken and birthed in the glory realm of heaven.

Approximately a year later, I was in intercession in the early morning hours. I had entered the glory realm and was laying prostrate under the weight of the atmosphere. I could see and hear Jesus. He stood and walked toward me. As He walked I could feel the wind of His robe. He was carrying a garment in His hand. Undone by this visitation, I remained face-down, weeping, but could see Him clearly in the Spirit. He spoke to me: "Becca, I am mantling you for the nations. You are one who will go to the nations, to the ends of the earth to stand in the land to see a harvest and transformation." As He spoke these words, He draped the mantle over me. It enveloped me much like a prayer shawl or tallit but had an anointing that was saturated with purpose. This is yet another life-changing moment with Him that forever united me to His plan.

Why do I share about these encounters? Because when you see Him and hear Him, life and circumstances as you know them oftentimes do not remain the same. His blueprint plan marks you for Kingdom purpose and presents you with the opportunity and invitation to partner with and step into His divine strategies and design. As stated so beautifully in Hebrews 1:3, "He is the radiance of the glory of God and the exact imprint of his nature, and he upholds the universe by the word of his power" (ESV). It was soon after these encounters that many prophetic words began to be spoken to me by others about the calling to the nations. I understood that in order to move forward I would have to learn about the truth of Kingdom authority and how to receive strategies for victory. This began a process of reading, many hours of intercession, delving deeper into the Word of God, and a life of discipline of encountering Him in the glory realm. I submitted myself under teachers and leaders who maneuver in undeniable glory-anointed spiritual authority, have wisdom in strategies for transformation, and who saw great victories in intercession and spiritual warfare prayer. Allow me to share significant truths I have learned.

POWER AND AUTHORITY

The Word of God tells us that we are heirs of God and co-heirs with Christ, that He has given us everything that pertains to life and godliness. This promise testifies to the fact that we are fellow participants in all that

He has made available in Kingdom of God. This also means that we are fellow partakers in the authority that is available as a son and daughter of the King of kings and Lord of lords. You see, when He entrusts us with assignments, He gives us power, which is the capacity to do and accomplish a task. This power is then empowered by our inherited Kingdom authority, which is the right to do and accomplish a task. You and I are called His ambassadors, ministers of reconciliation, more than conquerors. This is not only truth that He wants us to know in our minds, nor is it only contained as a law written on tablets of stone, but He has etched and written it through the Holy Spirit onto our hearts and into the very essence of who we are—our Kingdom identity. These are truths, spiritual realities, that cannot be shaken.

We are transformed into His image from glory to glory, and every encounter we have with Him will reveal different attributes of who He is and His greatness. We do not want to limit ourselves to just one or two or three of His attributes; we want to ascend into His throne room, into His glory, so that we can go deeper in Him. We can have as much of God as we want. The more He becomes our focus, the more we know Him and encounter Him, the more of His unending attributes will be unveiled. Our Lord and His Kingdom will not just be head knowledge that we are slightly acquainted with but a relationship that is secured and ignited in life-altering ways. And at some supernatural divine moment along this journey, His holiness and authority will be experienced in such holy reverence that you will know that you know He is a warrior King. When your warrior King speaks and entrusts assignments to you (even warfare assignments) in this glory realm, the sound of His voice will be engraved on your heart. The imprint of His voice that forever resounds in the Spirit, the authority that permeates the atmosphere, and the love will cause every cell in your being to exude His *ruach* breath. A certainty will be forged within you that the victory He has assured is yours. Heaven is filled with all power and authority. He is all power and authority.

And what is the surpassing greatness of His power toward us who believe, according to the working of His mighty power, which He performed in Christ when He raised Him from the dead and seated Him at His own right hand in the heavenly places, far above all principalities, and power, and might, and dominion, and every name that is named... (Ephesians 1:19-21).

It is in the atmosphere of heaven, in the glory realm, that all power and authority are married together.

When you receive this revelation, you will dare to go where no man has gone before to carry out that which He has decreed to be so. Glory realm revelation cannot be fathomed or contained in the human mind; it is a spirit-to-Spirit reality. These truths, friends, cannot be stripped away nor stolen.

ALL AUTHORITY HAS BEEN GIVEN

We can encounter Him. He is a warrior King. But what about authority? Jesus stated in Matthew 28:18, "All authority in heaven and on earth has been given to me" (NIV). He does not say *some* authority. He says *all* authority. The Greek word for "authority" is *exousia*, defined as authority to rule, jurisdiction, ruler, control, power, right to judge (Strong's #G1849). And if He has all authority and we are co-heirs in this authority, it means someone is missing it and does not have it.

Allow me to say this right here and now—satan is not God's equal. His evil and darkness are not equal to God's love and goodness. On the cross, Jesus disarmed, stripped off, disrobed, stripped away weapons of power and authority. However, satan is a sore, evil, angry, and vengeful loser. Therefore, he does implement schemes and strategies to keep us, our families, our cities, and our nations bound and hindered to keep our Lord's Kingdom from advancing. Paul gives this warfare lesson in Ephesians 6:11,

"Put on the whole armor of God that you may be able to stand against the schemes of the devil." The Greek word for "schemes" is *methodeia,* defined as scheming, craftiness, wiles, and strategies (Strong's #G3180). You see, satan has power to initiate evil plots, but he only has authority when mankind sins and engages in the demonic evil activities he is drawing us into, opening up a gate of influence to this dark prince.

I will state this observation now. Satan does initiate power strategies to kill, steal, and destroy, but it is rare to find those in the Church who have strategies to overcome and conquer. Hear me, friends. If satan and his army of darkness are continually about their business of implementing these evil schemes, then God will give us strategies to overcome and destroy these dark plots.

The Bible tells us we are "more than conquerors through Him who loved us" (Rom. 8:37 NKJV). Or an even more poignant way to express this is that the overwhelming victory or complete triumph is ours. Just as Paul was convinced beyond any doubt, we too should also be convinced, "that neither death, nor life, nor angels, nor principalities, nor things present and threatening, nor things to come, nor powers, nor height, nor depth, nor any other created thing, will be able to separate us from the [unlimited] love of God, which is in Christ Jesus our Lord" (Rom. 8:38-39 AMP). When we encounter Him and He imparts a strategy to us, there is peace, revelation, expectancy, determination, and joy as we begin to advance.

But doesn't the Word of God tell us that the battle is the Lord's? Yes. It does. It also tells us that our battle is not against flesh and blood, but rulers, principalities, spiritual hosts in the heavenly places. The Word of God further states that we are to resist the devil and he will flee from us. And that we are given authority to tread over serpents and scorpions and over all the power of the enemy. Spiritual authority will be discussed in depth in Chapter Eight, but I want to state plainly now that we are His ambassadors, His ministers of reconciliation, His Ekklesia with weapons of warfare. He has chosen us to be blood appropriators. The disciples turned the world upside down. We need to have the revelation of the authority we carry so we do not "yo-yo" or waver in our warfare. Darkness will not stop its onslaught but will take advantage of that moment. Moreover, God Himself is not in a fighting altercation with satan. He is God. He does not fight with angels, fallen angels, or demonic entities. He sends us as His armed and ready ones for battle to fight the enemy. And He dispatches His angel armies to do battle on our behalf and against the schemes of the enemy.

STRATEGIES FOR BATTLE

One thing I have seen repeatedly in over twenty-seven years of experience with prophecy, deliverance, prophetic intercession, and warfare assignments is that the Holy Spirit is always creative in how He speaks to us to engage. On a recent ministry trip to Scotland, we met a gentleman who had been trained and served in the Royal Marines, an amphibious troop of the Royal Navy, acknowledged as one of the world's elite commando forces. They are held at a very high readiness and can respond quickly to events anywhere around the globe. After hearing me teach, he handed Greg a sheet a paper with handwritten notes. It was the strategy used in battle procedures practiced by this branch of the military. It is interesting to see the how their strategy is similar to the strategies that the Lord has directed us to maneuver in. Let's take a closer look at each action step of this elite fighting force who have achieved overwhelming victory.

Advance to Contact

Seek Him and pursue Him for the assignment. There are principles of advancing and engagement that we can learn. However, do not get into the trap of allowing a method or rote prayer to always be your ammo. It is imperative to state—our Lord is creative, and the Holy Spirit always knows the best way to advance into breakthrough strategy. Therefore, it is my counsel to you as an intercessor to allow His voice and creative prophetic strategies to guide you through each of these military tactics.

Isaiah 60:1-2 gives great insight into the importance of glory encounters in receiving strategy to engage. "Arise, shine, for your light has come, and the glory of the Lord has risen upon you. For the darkness shall cover the earth and deep darkness the peoples; but the Lord shall rise upon you, and His glory shall be seen upon you." As a reminder, a few of the definitions and manifestations of the glory, *kabod,* include "manifestation of power, glorious presence, glory in the inner person, ruler, men of high rank, one who governs" (Strong's #H3519). This Scripture tells us the glory "shall be seen upon you." In other words, we will see a vision, find delight, find out, discover, give sight, meet with, advise, and have an encounter with a military head just prior to a fight between hostile military parties. As we are appointed for our assignment, the responsibility and anointing of that assignment rests upon us. The glory we are marked with is in virtual proximity to us. It reveals an opposition to darkness but ensures a strategy of an active, effective, operative responsibility to reach a goal and accomplish it.

Therefore, below are steps with brief descriptions of each that will aid you in the process of advancing to contact especially with assignments dealing with cities, regions, and nations. Many of these will be discussed throughout the remainder of the book. In-depth teaching on this topic is discussed in my book *Authority to Tread.*

1. **Form a team:** One crucial point our Royal Marine friend shared with us is the absolute necessity of team. The same is true in spiritual battles, and we firmly believe that in warfare prayer there are no lone rangers. Form a team who will function together in unity. Pray together, worship together. Ascend into His glory presence together. As a team, hear and receive His strategies to advance. Determine as a team how you will function in unity in the strategy that is forming. Spend time in team building.

2. **Research the history (spiritual mapping):** Discover how the enemy has taken what is not his. Have there been bloodshed, idolatry, pagan occult practices, covenant breaking, perversion, covenants made with darkness, God-robbing?

3. **Form a strategy from the prophetic revelation of the history of the region or gate of influence in which you are praying:** James 5:16 shares this truth, "The effective, fervent prayer of a righteous man avails much" (NKJV). To be effective we can't shoot or fire empty rounds into the enemy's camp. Combining prophecy and the research together anoints the assignment to be effective and hit the bull's eye.

4. **Intercessory prayer shield:** Mobilize intercessors who serve as a prayer shield to pray for your team.

5. **Seek the Lord for His timing on the assignment:** Only advance in the time He is leading you to advance. Advance when you and the team know the Lord has spoken the strategic time to be parachuted in.

Contact

I have led and will continue to lead times of corporate prophetic intercession. All families, ministries, and churches should have prayer as the foundation. I also believe that there is power in proximity. There is significant breakthrough that comes when we are on the land or standing at or within the gate of influence where the warfare assignment will occur. Sometimes even at this point, when you choose to show up atmospheres begin to shift. You will see the significance and importance of this in the testimony at the end of this chapter.

Engage the Enemy

You are now on site. It is time to do all that you have prepared to do. The definition of *engage* is to occupy, attract someone's attention, participate, move into position so as to come into operation, bring weapons together in preparation to fight. We are secure in the mindset and position that we will have impact and shift spiritual atmospheres.

All special forces have learned the art of knowing when to spy out, formulating a strategy, when to attack, and the building capability to possess. Special forces know how to be parachuted in and helicoptered out. They dare to go where no men dare to go, and they do it without interest in being known or seen. The majority of the time the most effective glory warfare strategies are done in a stealth manner.

One night I had a dream. In the dream I walked into a room and Doris Wagner was sitting in a chair. I approached her, sitting myself in the chair next to her. She looked intently at me and was very sure of what she spoke. She said several things, but I will share one statement. "To transform a nation in prayer, you must be hidden." What was the interpretation of these words? To be an effective intercessor who brings transformation, much of what you do will not be made known or made famous from a public platform. I can accurately state that where most transformational measures of breakthrough have occurred in a city, state, or nation there are stealth believers and intercessors who have engaged effectively without announcing the assignment to the masses. Ones who are anointed and marked for victorious warfare. All enemies fear these special forces, because it's not about personal fame but the fame of Jesus and His Kingdom.

Win the Firefight!

Now, as glory carriers and a Holy Spirit-appointed special ops brigade, it is time to advance in the assignment and win! This often will involve worship, reading Scripture, interceding through all the Lord has revealed, repenting for the sins that have occurred in the land, prophetic acts, prophetic proclamations, and decrees. Be expectant. Look for signs in the natural as you contend. Often, miracles are unfolding before our eyes.

Fight Through the Enemy's Position

One of the weaknesses that has occurred in the prayer movement is that we obtain a victory, but we must pray through the entire strategy to complete the assignment. Continue to obediently press through until you know the assignment has been accomplished. One assignment might involve multiple sites and locations.

Establish Safe Ground Beyond the Enemy's Position

Jeremiah 1:10 gives key ingredients to engage and build up: "See, I have appointed you this day over the nations and over the kingdoms, to uproot and break down, to destroy and to overthrow, to build and to plant" (AMP). Once we have received breakthrough, it is time to build and plant. Just as in deliverance ministry, the individual who has been set free is filled with the Holy Spirit; spheres of influence, lands, cities, and regions must also be filled with His glory and prophetic promises. Establish and build Kingdom centers that will steward and maintain the breakthrough—ones that will plant and develop a deep spiritual root system and presence. This might be establishing 24/7 prayer, establishing a location that provides an apostolic and prophetic Kingdom expression, initiating involvement and action in all spheres of society and culture, and impacting the region in revival and transformation. The beauty of this victory for those in the region is that they will reap the benefits and lasting fruit of the freedom and victory that the special ops team has obtained. They might not have engaged in the firefight, but they are the ones who will enjoy and live in the winnings of the special elite force. There must be those in the region who continue to pour into, maintain, build, and plant now that it is set free from the schemes of the enemy.

Ammunition and Casualty Count

Stay in communication with your team and those in the region after completing the assignment to ensure each one is not experiencing backlash.

Continue to have the intercessors provide a covering and prayer shield for the team and those established in the region. Don't glorify what the enemy will do. Watch the news media, read the papers, stay in touch with those in the land to receive updated reports of tangible breakthrough because of the engagement in the region. Look for and expect results.

Don't Get Prideful

Be careful of pride. Do not become prideful because of the breakthroughs that have been achieved. Pride always comes before a fall and will be a red-carpet invitation to come under the defensive fire from the enemy. You can't stand still in the enemy's position, patting yourself on the back. Remember, it is the Lord who receives the glory for the breakthrough that has occurred.

WHEN TIME STOOD STILL

The year was 2013. I was leading a team of eight awesome prayer warriors to the nation of Spain. We have been traveling into this nation since 2004, partnering with key leaders Jose and Elba Lopez. Over the past 14 years we have driven over 9,000 miles across the peninsula praying for revival, breakthrough, and transformation.

The focus of this assignment was to pray from France, across Spain, and into Portugal along the path of empowerment established by the Knights Templar. If you are unfamiliar with this group, they are the ones who established the foundation for the banking system in the nations of the world. They were warriors and fought many battles that at the core were unrighteous. The control of people, violence, and the wealth of nations was the foundation of this organization, which resulted in corrupt banking systems entrenched with occult practices.

The strategy the Lord revealed to us was to pray along this trail crossing these three nations. The focus was to engage at key strategic locations where they practiced occult forms of worship and caused immense bloodshed through warfare to empower the idolatrous structures they revered. How did we know this was our assignment? The Lord specifically spoke to us that 2014 was the time to address the foundation of the banking system that was and still is influencing financial institutions in the world.

One key location we were to visit was the ancient castle in a beautiful, historic, sleepy town of Miravet. As is normal, all the castles were built on high places. After praying, we looked over the city from that high place and prophesied, calling in a harvest of souls as there are no Christian churches in this town. We also called for a release of hidden wealth. The Lord highlighted the steeple of an old cathedral and several team members felt we should pray there. Some walked down the steep trail to the center of town while I, Brandon, and Kate Larson drove the van.

Arriving at the parking lot, we exited the van to proceed to the cathedral. However, I saw an advertisement that pictured Magnum ice cream bars. For me this has proven to be a great temptation. No discussion needed! Instead of walking uphill to the cathedral, I instantly made my way into the store to make my purchase. The gentleman behind the counter, Aurelio, welcomed us with a warm smile and began communicating in Spanish. I am able to speak a few words in Spanish, but I am not fluent. Yet when he spoke, I was supernaturally able to respond almost fluently. Soon, it was evident that this was paving the way for a friendly conversation to ensue. After a few minutes of "Spanglish," the rest of the team made their way into the entrance of the store, explaining that the cathedral doors were locked.

The owner of the store inquired, "Are you wanting to visit the new or the old cathedral?"

In unison we responded, "The old cathedral." He explained it was not open for tours. Taking the opportunity of my newfound friendship, I shared we were only visiting Miravet that day and were highly interested in visiting this ancient site. "Is there someone you know who could help us gain access?"

He responded, "You must know the keeper of the keys."

This quickly caused our prophetic ears to come to attention. Feeling the leading of the Holy Spirit, I asked, "Do you know the keeper of the keys?"

Smiling, he replied, "Yes. It's me. I am the keeper of the keys."

Excitement and laughter began to break out among the team as I took the opportunity to step further into our newfound favor, "Will you take us to the cathedral?" He gladly agreed, but we would have to wait thirty minutes allowing him time to close the store for siesta. Aurelio learned we had not eaten lunch and made a reservation with a restaurant in town for 3:15 P.M. to follow the tour. As we began the journey on the uphill road leading to the cathedral, the time was 2:20 P.M.

It was quickly evident that he was not only a store owner and the keeper of the keys, but also a top-notch historian. I must state that when you are obedient and step out in faith, God will ensure you relate to the right person, at the right place, at the right time. However, what should have been a ten-minute walk turned into thirty minutes as he shared the history of every block and building. When we arrived at the cathedral and made our way through the now unlocked and opened door, I glanced at my watch. It was 2:55 p.m. I thought all plans for our lunch appointment would be foiled. Brandon was also checking the time. We exchanged glances acknowledging the situation. However, both of us having been in supernatural experiences knew this was a divine setup. Therefore, we did not voice our concern; we allowed what we sensed was a supernatural divine encounter to unfold.

The inside of the cathedral was dusty, old, dilapidated. It had been through many battles without repair. Aurelio soon directed his conversation and attention to the front of the room. In the center of the altar was an old stone table. He invited all eight of us to gather around. He shared, "I feel I need to tell you things I do not normally share. You look as if you are people in the know, so I will tell you what I know." Expectantly we all leaned over the stone altar, pressing closer to listen. He proceeded to share the history of the Knights Templar in the region, information about their occult practices, and their involvement in sacred geometry. The altar we were circling was the only remaining occult altar of the eight Knights Templar altars used in the ancient Iberian Peninsula before they were disbanded by the King of France in 1312. Many of the Templars were welcomed into London and fled to that city. In time, several returned to collect all eight altars. They were able to locate seven but were unable to find the one housed in Miravet. The townspeople did not want to give up this sacred relic and retrieved it from the castle. They moved it into the cathedral, and it has been hidden since that time.

In recent history, the Templars had learned of the altar's location. Instead of moving it to the museum in London where the other seven altars are displayed, the decision was made to leave it in Miravet, its town of origin. However, in February of 2014, a group of high-ranking Knights Templar, those who are "in the know," had returned to reactivate the power of the altar. Due to his trusted position as keeper of the keys, our friend, Aurelio, was invited to witness the occult ritual. He explained what occurred at midnight on that February night. The occult ceremony included chanting in a demonic sound to reactivate the witchcraft empowerment of the altar to influence Miravet, the nation of Spain, and the nations of the world. This occult brotherhood believes that in their occult powers they can produce wealth and metals in the atmosphere through the sound of their chanting. It is their intent to manipulate time, causing it to stand still to accomplish victory in battles and fulfill all the tasks necessary to control wealth. Friends, these practices are evil and demonic. I know this sounds a little "out there," but all these revelations I am sharing with you are historically and factually accurate. Jareb, a team member, planned for several of us to speak with the highest-ranking active Knights Templar who is also a highly respected historian. He travels and speaks about the history and practices of this organization. All of what I am sharing in this testimony he openly shared with us to be true.

The team was now beyond excited. We had been sent on assignment by the Lord to another nation to pray and contend against the power of this system influencing the wealth in the world. God so orchestrated our steps that we were now standing around the only ancient active altar of this occult group. To make a long story shorter, several of our team members were able to pray around that altar while several of us continued to speak to Aurelio in another room. Before leaving the cathedral, Aurelio expressed his desire to give us a gift. He positioned himself in front of that occult altar and began to beautifully sing an ancient Latin chorus, glorifying the magnificence and holiness of God. This moment was a divine setup which paved the way for me to offer Aurelio a gift. I too positioned myself in front of the demonic altar. As a worship warfare act to break the power of the demonic sound that had been released from that altar, I sang "Amazing Grace." The tangible glory of God fell in that temple and the darkness of that ancient stronghold was broken. Aurelio along with each of the team members and I wept tears in His glorious presence.

After our lengthy time in the cathedral, it was time for him to return to the store. As we departed, I glanced at my watch, feeling confident that we had missed our lunch appointment. To my utter surprise the time was 3:00 P.M. Could it really be possible that only five minutes had passed? Surely this wasn't right. Brandon was also in the same evaluating process. Without speaking a word, we both knew what had just occurred. We arrived at the restaurant exactly on time at 3:15 P.M. I waited until the team was seated at the table. There was much excitement concerning the miracle of the Lord making a way for us to pray at an altar when two hours before we had no knowledge of its existence. I asked the team members to look at their watches and share the time. They gladly obliged. I then explained, "When we walked into that cathedral it was 2:55 P.M. When we walked out it was 3:00 P.M. Time just stood still for us."

Jareb then replied, "Becca, when I realized the full history lesson we were receiving from Aurelio I decided to record him. The time of the recording on my tablet is 45 minutes." Weeping broke out across that table. When you are anointed for an assignment in the glory realm and you receive His strategies, He will be with you in every step from the beginning to the end—advance to contact, make contact, engage the enemy, win the firefight, push through the enemy's position, establish safe ground beyond the enemy's position, ensure the enemy's weapons are removed. Trust me, He will get you to the right place at the right time to ensure the assignment is completed through to victory.

CHAPTER FIVE

ASSIGNED FOR VICTORY

Through you I ascend to the highest peaks of your glory
to stand in the heavenly places, strong and secure in
you. You've trained me with the weapons of warfare-
worship; now I'll descend into battle with power to
chase and conquer my foes. You empower me for victory
with your wrap-around presence. Your power within
makes me strong to subdue, and by stooping down in
gentleness you strengthened me and made me great!
—Psalm 18:33-35 TPT

One night when I was up late in intercession, the Lord spoke the following word to me. "Becca if you stay in a *metron* that I am no longer calling you to or asking you to stay in, then you are out of My best assignment for that season. Be who you are. You be you. Be where I am calling you to be."

What is the meaning of *metron?* To further understand, a quick study of Second Corinthians 10:12-13 will give us a clear understanding:

We do not have the audacity to put ourselves in the same class or compare ourselves with some who [supply testimonials to] commend themselves. When they measure themselves by themselves and compare themselves with themselves, they lack wisdom and behave like fools. We, on the other hand, will not boast beyond our proper limit, but [will keep] within the limits of our commission (territory, authority) which God has granted to us as a measure, which reaches and includes even you (AMP).

The Greek word for "measure" is *metron*. It means to cut out a space or distance with a measurer's reed or rule (Strong's #G3358). It refers to the size or boundary of one's area of authority. The Greek word for "rule" is *kanon,* which signifies a sphere of activity (Strong's #G2583). It refers to the power one has within a certain marked-out territory. To gain further understanding, the word for "grant" or "distribute" is *merizo,* which is speaking of a division or share (Strong's #G3307). Putting this together, we can see that Paul was teaching that the Lord allots specific areas, callings, authority, spheres of influence for each of us as His children in which we can move in power and authority and make known the Kingdom of God. The same principle applies to you and me. It is exciting to gain the insight and revelation that the Lord has given to each of us a portion on earth over which we have been assigned to effect change, bring His presence, and see transformation come.

This concept should not be entirely unfamiliar to us. I believe at some point in our lives we have all experienced this godly authority—a time when we discovered an innate ability and empowerment to lead or a time when righteous indignation rose up in our spirits and brought necessary changes. It might not be a regular occurrence, but there are times when unjust situations present themselves and something within us takes charge in the circumstance at hand. This is the power and authority rising up in our Kingdom identity. The more time you spend in the Word, in His presence and in the glory, the more you discover that in moments as just described, He will move through you powerfully and effectively in ways that you could not have worked up or accomplished on your own.

KNOW YOUR ASSIGNMENTS

There is an important principle in knowing His assignments for the seasons we are in, especially warfare assignments. Being in the assignment begets authority for victory and breakthrough. The truth is, if we take on assignments that have not been allotted to us, we can wear ourselves out by striving in order to make things happen and begin to feel worn down, battle weary. I have seen this happen with many leaders and prayer warriors over the years. They take on every assignment that is discerned without seeking Him over the specific missions He is calling them to. Time is not spent in His glory presence to hear and receive clearly the marching orders to advance in order to achieve victory.

Then there is the mental battle that oftentimes we think we have to be perfect before adventuring into a new season. So many great men and women of God had obstacles to press through. They weren't picture perfect candidates for their Kingdom assignments. Moses stuttered. Abraham and Sarah were beyond childbearing years. Rahab was a prostitute. Timothy was young. Martha was too busy. Peter denied Jesus. Paul, when he was Saul, killed Christians. Deborah was a woman fighting in a man's army.

Oh, and what about David? Let's take this moment to study this key leader and history maker. He was the youngest and least likely of his brothers to be chosen, anointed, and appointed as king of Israel, but nevertheless he was the one designated by God. He was anointed by Samuel, but the moment of anointing did not instantly lead him to the throne. There were seasons of growth and new assignments he had to experience and grow into. We know he was a gifted musician as his music calmed Saul in the demonic torment he was enduring. He was a brave shepherd and slew a lion and a bear with a sling shot. He had been prepared in the place of worship and in the midst of the fields facing off the fierce wild animals. He grew in the exact gifts God would use while he walked through the process of ascending to the throne.

This leads us to the historic moment with Goliath, the uncircumcised Philistine, who dared to challenge and mock the army of Israel and to defy God. Truthfully, this battle was not just focused on conquering a cruel, antagonistic giant who towered over the smaller stature of David. It wasn't a physical battle that made defeating Goliath so amazing—although it was a miraculous feat. David was running fearlessly and boldly head-on into a battle against the culture of a people known as the enemy of the children of Israel. Yes, Goliath was a giant, but he also represented the very essence of a culture that was ruthless at its core. The Philistines were a proud people. They were heavily steeped in idolatrous worship. They were extremely superstitious and blatantly warlike. Their mission was to oppress God's chosen people. Remember, they attempted to steal the ark, God's presence, from the temple. And they attempted to mix God's presence with a demonic entity by the name of dagon. Listen to this powerful Scripture about how the Lord responds and reacts to those who mock Him: "But they continually mocked the messengers of God, despised His words and scoffed at His prophets, until the wrath of the Lord arose against His people, until there was no remedy" (2 Chron. 36:16 NASB).

Even in the midst of this giant mocking and defying God and Israel, all the men in the army were afraid of Goliath and the impending threat of the invasion of the Philistine army and culture in order to make them slaves. Friends, David was a teenager—seventeen years old. He was physically too small to slay Goliath, a giant who towered over nine feet tall. Even when David was moving in faith to accept the challenge of taking on Goliath, his own brother, Eliab, mocked him and his motives. This leads me to a valid point in warfare. Isn't it interesting that Eliab judged the condition of David's heart and motives in his ordained time of faith and favor to defeat this terrorizing foe? If you remember, the Lord shared with Samuel when he inquired if Eliab was the one to be anointed, "Do not look on his appearance or on the height of his stature, because I have rejected him. For the Lord sees not as man sees. For man looks on the outward appearance, but the Lord looks on the heart" (1 Sam. 16:7). The area that disqualified Eliab from becoming king is the exact area he attempted to publicly judge, ridicule, and mock David. He claimed his heart was full of pride and evil—that his motives were not pure (see 1 Sam. 17:28).

It is evident that David had several things working against him at this crucial moment—his age, size, his own brother publicly mocking him and questioning the motives of his heart, lack of military experience, and this giant ruthlessly intimidating him declaring his victory over David and his certain death. Even so, in his age, physical limitations, and public ridicule he chose to believe in the strength and vastness of God rather than to focus on his own limited stature and fighting experience. The warrior in David rose up, he acted, and his words declared:

> You come to me with a sword, a spear, and a javelin, but I come to you in the name of the Lord of hosts, the God of the armies of Israel, whom you have taunted. This day the Lord will hand you over to me, and I will strike you down and cut off your head. And I will give the corpses of the army of the Philistines this day to the birds of the sky and the wild beasts of the earth, so that all the earth may know that there is a God in Israel, and that this entire assembly may know that the Lord does not save with the sword or with the spear; for the battle is the Lord's and He will hand you over to us (1 Samuel 17:45-47 AMP).

Shortening this in modern vernacular, David decreed, "*Challenge accepted!*" He saw at that moment that God in him was bigger than that giant. And somehow, in that moment, he knew that if he fought on behalf of God and His name he would have that victory. He threw that stone from that sling shot and hit Goliath dead center in the forehead, killing him instantly. To exact and ensure this bold victory, he cut off his head. David the shepherd boy—anointed to be king, lion slayer, bear slayer, psalmist, worship-warrior—defeated the giant, leading to the ultimate defeat of the enemy of Israel. My point in this—slaying Goliath was David's assignment! He knew the battle was ordained by God and made sure that everyone, including his enemy, knew this battle was ordained by God. He got in the fight, dedicating it to the Lord: "The battle belongs to the Lord." So, friends, never allow your limitations or the lies the enemy speaks to you about your limitations to determine your future or the victory. God is bigger. Way, way bigger.

WE DO WHAT WE SEE AND HEAR THE FATHER DOING

Jesus taught us the way to know which assignments we are to carry out. He models and teaches us through His own example that He does what He sees His Father doing. Jesus focused His ministry on responding to His Father. His ministry was not reactive to what satan was doing. Jesus was anointed to carry out His Father's assignments, and it was from that surrendered place that the glory, anointed power, and authority exuded from Jesus and caused darkness to react and expose itself. Friends, this is where our union with the Lord is so vital—time in His presence and glory to hear and to know beyond any doubt what He has destined you to do. If it was necessary for Jesus to pull away, pray, seek His Father's voice, then you and I will have to do that same thing.

Think of the transfiguration. Jesus was transformed into His glorified body while talking with Elijah and Moses who also appeared in their glorified state. Why was the meeting of the three so significant? In this glory encounter, Moses was representing the Old Covenant and Elijah the prophets. Jesus was the fulfillment of the prophecies and the law. Culminating on the cross, the Kingdom design was confirmed and married to shape the history of the world. This occurred in the glory realm but was carried out and made manifest in the land and on the earth. Jesus had to defeat satan and his army of darkness on the earth. I will say it again—Jesus, the Son of God and man, was anointed in a heavenly encounter, the glory realm, in which He was transfigured. He carried out and secured the victory on earth. Why? Because this is where satan and his army of darkness are roaming, seeking whom they may devour. Ever since they were kicked out of heaven, this demonic army engages their warfare in the second heaven or spirit realm of supernatural activity positioned between the earth and heaven, and they roam the earth, the land, seeking whom they may devour.

Establishing a Foundation

Just as David and Jesus secured great victories, in our lives we can learn and implement the dynamic resolve they both maneuvered in to contend for victory. There are foundational principles we can glean from these testimonies and the Scriptures to know how each of us, you and I, can maneuver in life and intercession as God's soldier.

Maturing in Holiness

> Holiness is not to love Jesus and do whatever you want. Holiness is to love Jesus and do what He wants.[1]

To be effective warriors, holiness is essential. Most leaders agree on this foundational truth but choose to stay at a more elementary level of holiness. However, the Lord wants each of us to learn how to mature in holiness becoming more and more like Him. Then there are those who go to the extreme and teach that holiness is the end goal of everything. The focus becomes on polishing Christians to such an extent that this high level of ministry will flow out of them. We absolutely want to always grow and mature in holiness. But if we are only focusing on ourselves continually, making ourselves better, this can turn into a "bless me" mentality.

Remember, as stated in the discussion about Eliab, the holiness of the heart or inward holiness is key in this maturing process.

Indicators that someone has issues in maturing in holiness include habitually using the Lord's name in vain, engaging in sexual sin, falsifying financial reports, addictions of any kind, lying, unforgiveness, abusive anger, and murder, just to name a few. The issues must be repented of. And if they become sin patterns and strongholds, receiving deliverance ministry is vital to overcome. Hear me—do not accept a life of demonic bondage and strongholds as normal. Overcome and defeat them.

On the other hand, if we wait until we attain perfection to begin to move forward in our Christian life, then none of us would ever begin to move forward. The beauty is we can ask the Lord daily to help keep us from temptation. He will guide and help you in this. And we begin to reflect and to become like that which we behold. The more we behold Him, the more our hearts' desire will grow to be like Him. And we can move beyond where we have been into what is to be.

Humility

"The fear of the Lord is the beginning of wisdom" (Ps. 111:10). The fear of the Lord will keep us focused, sober-minded, and free from many harmful situations. Proverbs 22:4 also shares that, "True humility and fear of the Lord lead to riches, honor, and long life" (NLT). In Chapter Four, I shared my first encounter with Jesus in His throne room. It was a holy moment that brought me into the reality of how awesome and majestic He really is. There are those times when He allows us to encounter Him in His holiness, and in that place you bow low in humility, respect, and honor. The magnitude of His greatness should not be taken lightly. Coming into a place of humility in our walk is so very key.

Obedience to Him

We must lay down our agendas and oftentimes sacrifice time and entertainment to draw closer to Him. The truth is, if we want to be anointed in the glory for breakthrough and victory, we have to spend time in His Word and in His presence to receive the strategies and authority that cause darkness to flee. Keep your gaze fixed on Jesus. Pursue Him. Seek Him. Stay in His Word. Continue in obedience. Do not lose heart. Choose joy. He who began a good work will be faithful to complete it. Through Him we are being transformed from glory to glory. Abide, stay vitally connected to Him, and our joy will be made complete in Him.

> Obedience calls for courage. Courage is the resolve to obey despite what we feel. Exercise your trust in God by stepping out in obedience. "Be strong and courageous. Do not fear or be in dread of them, for it is the Lord your God who goes with you. He will not leave you or forsake you" (Deuteronomy 31:6).[2]

The following is a powerful truth often spoken by Arthur Burke: "100,000 little choices releases you into an epic moment of earned authority." Friends, all your little yeses to Him and your yeses to obedience to Him will carry you into an epic moment of earned authority. Do you have epic moment stories? We do and we want more. One epic moment of earned authority in His Kingdom can radically transform and shape history. That epic moment can get you where you thought it was impossible to go. It will open doors that no one can shut. And can move you into such supernatural moments that you thought could only be read about in His Word. All of your little yeses release you into epic supernatural moments much like what occurred in the Book of Acts. So, do your one little yes today, and do your two little yeses the next day, and you keep doing those little yeses every day and watch for the epic moment of earned authority and the resulting victories achieved. Say yes to Him!

Honor

Honor brings the glory. If you do not honor then you will not experience glory, the supernatural, or victorious breakthrough. What does the word *honor* mean? In the Bible it carries many meanings. I do find it interesting that one of the prominent definitions of honor in the Bible is also glory or to make glorious (Strong's #H3513). It also signifies respect, strength, authority, esteem, value, and integrity. I appreciate the wisdom expressed by John Bevere:

> The simplistic and literal definition of *time* (honor) is "a valuing." When you speak of the word *time* to a Greek man, he thinks of something *valuable, precious, weighty*, such as gold. Think of it—you don't put gold in your junk drawer; rather you assign it to a place of honor. Other definitions of honor are *appreciation, esteem, favorable, regard, respect*.
>
> From looking at my study of Greek dictionaries and commentaries I've discovered that honor can be displayed in action, word, and even thought. But all true honor originates from the heart. This is why God says, "Inasmuch as these people draw near with their mouths *and honor Me with their lips*, but have *removed their hearts far from Me*, and their *fear toward Me* is taught by the commandment of men (Isa. 29:13, emphasis mine).[3]

The Bible teaches the importance of honor in many areas of relationships in our lives. The following are a few scriptural directives.

- Paul encourages us to, "Honor your mother and father... so that it might go well with you and you enjoy long life on the earth" (Eph. 6:2-3 NIV).

- Peter tells us in First Peter 2:17, "Honor all people, love the brotherhood, fear God, honor the king" (NASB). We are to show esteem, respect and honor to all people including those in authority, such as a king.

- Paul teaches in First Timothy 5:17, "The elders who rule well are to be considered worthy of double honor, espe-

cially those who work hard at teaching and preaching"
(NASB).

- He further explains the importance of honor in our
  work relationships and environments. It is valuable to
  remember even in the workplace we are an example of
  the Kingdom to all we encounter.

*Those who are employed should listen to their employers
and obey their instructions with great respect and honor.
Serve them with humility in your hearts as though you were
working for the Master* (Ephesians 6:5 TPT).

- We are to show honor, love, and devotion in our mar-
  riages, as so clearly stated in Ephesians 5:23-25:

*For the husband provides leadership for the wife, just as Christ
provides leadership for his church, as the Savior and Reviver
of the body. In the same way the church is devoted to Christ,
let the wives be devoted to their husbands in everything. And
to the husbands, you are to demonstrate love for your wives
with the same tender devotion that Christ demonstrated to
us, his bride. For he died for us, sacrificing himself* (TPT).

- Fathers and (I would like to add) mothers should raise
  their children in love, which teaches honor and draws
  them to the Lord.

*Fathers, don't exasperate your children but raise them up
with loving discipline and counsel that brings the revelation
of our Lord* (Ephesians 6:4 TPT).

- Most importantly, we are to show all honor to the Lord.

*You are worthy, our Lord and God, to receive glory, honor,
and power, for you created all things, and by your plan they
were created and exist* (Revelation 4:11 TPT).

Honor is a character trait that is greatly missing in the world today. But we as believers should set the example and the standard. I find it interesting the highest medal given in the military is the Medal of Honor. It is given to those who live a life of honor. As cited in the Army Values, "Honor is a matter of carrying out, acting, and living the values of respect, duty, loyalty, selfless service, integrity and personal courage in everything you do."[4] If we are going to be victorious warriors in the Kingdom of God we must be an army dedicated to living an exemplary life of honor, respect, and esteem.

Determination

Determined soldiers carry a firmness in purpose because of a resolve in Christ. As a further scriptural example, Ruth expressed this determination to stay with Naomi. As stated in Ruth 1:18, "When Naomi saw that she [Ruth] was determined to go with her, she said no more to her." David was determined to see Goliath and the Philistines defeated. No matter what or who tried to stop him, he was determined and did not shrink back.

Courage

Courage means that even when we are unsure we will face those fears, let go of our fears, and advance without any evidence of fear. Courage gives us the ability to stand under the greatest persecution and pressure. To have the courage to stand true to one's convictions. To act according to one's beliefs even in the face of criticism. Another great description of courage is backbone, the ability to stand firm.

High Morale

Being in high praise, worship, thanksgiving. Having the spirit of a cheerleader. Being expectant and praising the Lord in the midst of the battle through to the victory. Those of you who know me and have heard me teach have become familiar with my common exclamation of "Woohoo!" I jokingly say that *woohoo* is Texan for "praise God." Hear me—spiritual warfare is not about flexing our spiritual muscles. This is not why we do it.

I have to admit the story of David and Goliath is a little bloody and gory, but I am sure there was praise, thanksgiving, and celebration in response to this victory—a big *woohoo* resounding in the hearts and spirits of the children Israel. The enemy who came to defeat and enslave them as a nation was overcome and defeated.

Devotion

A devoted life is an immeasurable dedication to the cause. David issued the challenge in First Samuel 17:29, "Is there not a cause?" (NKJV). When God gives a cause to fight for there will be that dedication to stand and fight for the cause to see victory come.

Tenacity

This is the ability to retain and hold on to what is true. It is a firm grabbing hold of that which God is imparting and not letting it out of your grip.

Persistence

Knowing what is true and right. The determination to continue to insist on what is right. David was persistent in his stance against this Philistine. There was a persistent righteous indignation that rose up in David that refused to allow the mocking, defying words and actions of Goliath to rule the day.

Resolve

A formal resolution means that the truths pertaining to God are settled in your heart without any ifs, ands, or buts. In order to contend, you cannot waiver in what the Lord has asked of you to do.

Readiness

Be ready in season and out of season. To be ready you must be consistent in reading and feasting on His Word and have the mentality of being available anytime He calls for the assignment at hand.

Team Mentality

Realize it takes a team. To be effective in battle you have to be a team player. Understand and realize that each voice, gift, and person on the team is necessary and valuable to achieve the victory. Esteeming others is key. "Do nothing from factional motives [through contentiousness, strife, selfishness, or for unworthy ends] or prompted by conceit and empty arrogance. Instead, in the true spirit of humility (lowliness of mind) let each regard the others as better than and superior to himself [thinking more highly of one another than you do of yourselves]" (Phil. 2:3 AMPC). Choose to walk in unity, and understand when to defer and when to step out.

WHAT WILL IT COST YOU?

The night the Lord asked me this question is still very vivid in my memory. I had submitted my name for the first time to participate on a warfare prayer journey. The trip was to Nigeria. The church we were attending required those interested in participating to fill out an application and go through an interview process. It was several nights before the interview. I was in intercession until the wee hours of the morning. The Lord began to speak to me yet again about spiritual warfare prayer and the nations. He asked, *"Are you willing to travel to the nations of the earth to pray?"* I responded, "Yes, Lord." He asked, *"Are you willing to follow Me no matter the cost?"* I answered, "Lord, I want to say yes. Help me to have the strength to say yes." He then asked, *"Do you love not your life unto death?"* Unto death? How in the world would I answer this question? I wanted so badly to tell Him that I was willing to give my life, but an intense struggle was going on inside of me.

Over the next few days, I began to cry out to the Lord to give me the strength to follow Him no matter the cost. The night before my scheduled interview, I was able to answer God and tell Him that I wanted to follow Him no matter the cost. I asked Him to give me the strength to do this. It was a powerful time of prayer, and I thought that I had resolved this issue in my spirit.

I went for the interview the next day and things were proceeding well. As the last question was asked, I understood why the struggle of the previous few days had occurred. Alice Smith looked right at me and asked, "Are you willing to give your life for the Lord?"

I answered, "I knew you were going to ask that question. I have been before the Lord the past few days and crying out for the strength to say yes. The best that I can answer is I have told the Lord that I desire to follow Him no matter the cost and have asked Him to give me the strength to do so." Even though I was not chosen as a team member for this trip, the Lord used this process to prepare me for future warfare assignments. It was a time in my life of deep soul searching and truly laying my life agendas before the Lord and accepting His plan for my life.

I really felt that this was a resolved issue until a few months later. Our pastor was preaching a message that pierced my heart. He began to challenge the congregation to deeper commitment and shared incredible stories from *Foxe's Book of Martyrs* of men and women who were faithful to the Lord until the end. I knew as he preached this inspiring message that I had not completely resolved the issue. Day after day I got on my knees before the Lord and cried out, "Lord, make me faithful to the end." I had weighed the cost and wanted to commit fully so that I could go to the nations. The nations were then and still are burning in my heart. I told no one, not even my husband, about this burden. It was between me and God.

Three weeks into this time with the Lord, I attended a meeting for the intercessors who prayed regularly for Eddie and Alice Smith. The Lord had told Alice to bless their intercessors in this meeting. She began to pray and prophesy over each of us. As she looked at me she called my name and pointed her finger toward me. It felt as if the Lord were standing in front of me. She looked right in my eyes and declared, "The Lord says you will be faithful to the end!" That word shot through me with like a glory bolt of lightning. It penetrated every part of my being. I began to tremble. She then said, "The Lord has given you this word, so when you are in intense situations you can grab hold of it and know that you will be faithful no matter the cost."

After that evening, the Lord began to release me into strategic level spiritual warfare prayer. I began to experience deeper levels of glory intercession in my prayer closet. Invitations were extended to participate in prophetic warfare assignments in Houston, Texas, our nation, and the nations. Truthfully, I can state that I have been in intense and dangerous situations since this word was spoken to me. Because this word is alive in my spirit, I do not allow fear to keep me from moving forward and pressing into the call the Lord has placed on my life.

Right now, you might feel this is a bit weighty. I want to express that following after Jesus is a pure joy. He is my destination. And what I lay down for Him, I do not consider loss. Why? Because to have more of Him is unending gain. And He might not ask this level of surrender of everyone reading this book. However, because I am called to nations and sometimes dangerous places, this was an issue the Lord required me to resolve in my heart.

On the other hand, I can also hear in my spirit as I type these words, *the nations are calling.* Some of you may be feeling this even as you read. I want to encourage you to say yes to the Lord, surrender to Him all that He is requiring, come into the abiding place in His glory, and be like David. Align yourself with those who can mentor you into a fullness of destiny. When He calls you to contend, let the cry of *challenge accepted* rise in your spirit and resound out of your mouth into the atmosphere. Do not shrink back; advance as He leads you in His blueprint plan and be expectant of the victory that will unfold. We are not anointed in the glory for defeat, but He will want a resolve that you will follow no matter what the cost.

CREATION IS WAITING FOR YOU!

*Praise the Lord from the earth, sea monsters and all
deeps; lightning and hail, snow and fog; stormy wind,
fulfilling His orders; mountains and all hills; fruitful
trees and all cedars; beasts and all cattle; creeping things
and winged birds; kings of the earth and all people;
princes and all judges of the earth; both young men
and virgins; old men and children. Let them praise the
name of the Lord, for His name alone is exalted and
supreme; His glory and majesty are above earth and
heaven. He has lifted up a horn for His people [giving
them strength, prosperity, dignity, and preeminence],
praise for all His godly ones; for the people of Israel, a
people near to Him. Praise the Lord!* (**HALLELUJAH!**)
—PSALM 148:7–14 AMP*

Praise God from the earth! What a powerful Scripture. It is evident throughout the Word of God that creation responds to our creator King. Creatures, the elements, the trees, rocks, stars, creeping things, birds, men, women, all mankind. All creatures respond when they hear the voice of their Creator. A few more scriptural examples to aid us in this study:

> *Then the trees of the forest will ring out before the Lord, for He is coming to judge the earth* (1 Chronicles 16:33).

> *Let the field be joyful, and all that is in it; then all the trees of the forests shall rejoice* (Psalm 96:12).

> *By them the birds of the heavens have their habitation; they sing among the branches* (Psalm 104:12).

One of the more poignant Scriptures sharing this truth is Habakkuk 2:14: "The earth will be filled the knowledge of the glory of the Lord." *Knowledge* means to know, realize, to become known, become aware of, familiar with, a friend of. In other words, the earth will be filled with the intimate knowledge of His glory. And within this promise there is a personal invitation offered to each of us. As discussed in Chapter Four, you and I are glory carriers marked with His glory in order that it can be seen on us and manifested through us to advance His Kingdom.

LEAVING OUR MARK

You and I are to engage in such a way that we leave a Kingdom mark, a glory imprint on peoples, spheres, and lands. Great weight is carried on how we choose to live our lives, how we faithfully pray, war, contend, and gain victories. As Jesus made known, "Blessed are the meek, for they shall inherit the earth" (Matt. 5:5). This earth, this land upon which our feet tread is our inheritance. But isn't this a future tense of what we will obtain with Jesus? The answer is yes; however, let's look at the beginning, the middle, and the end in order to fully grasp what our heavenly Father has made available to us as our inheritance.

God created man to partner with Him in creation.

> Then God said, "Let Us (Father, Son, Holy Spirit) make man in Our image, according to Our likeness [not physical, but a spiritual personality and moral likeness]; and let them have complete authority over the fish of the sea, the birds of the air, the cattle, and over the entire earth, and over everything that creeps and crawls on the earth." So God created man in His own image, in the image and likeness of God He created him; male and female He created them. And God blessed them [granting them certain authority] and said to them, "Be fruitful, multiply, and fill the earth, and subjugate it [putting it under your power]; and rule over (dominate) the fish of the sea, the birds of the air, and every living thing that moves upon the earth" (Genesis 1:26-28 AMP).

What does this God breathed and destined inheritance mean for us? The Hebrew word for rule is *radah*; it means to lead, control (Strong's #H7287). It means that we are a people and/or government with certain authority that has been granted to us. "Subdue," *kabas*, means to overcome, conquer, control (Strong's #H3533). It is apparent that these words carry significant meaning and weight. I am not telling everyone to go out and take over the world in a dominating manner. However, I will say this—our Creator is the everlasting God of the universe for all eternity. His Kingdom never ends. As His created sons and daughters who have been blessed to rule and reign with Him in the earth, we must not think of this inheritance in a less-than manner of "that was for then" or "this is our future. It does not apply now." On the contrary, it does absolutely apply now and forevermore.

The Hebrew word for "bless" is *barak*. It means to kneel down, to adore with bended knee, that God blessed man as His benefit (Strong's #H1288).

Mankind are the ones to advance, commend, speak words invoking divine favor with the intent that the object will have favorable circumstances. When God created Adam and Eve, the earth was full of endless inheritance in relationship with Him, and they were to steward that which He created and positioned them in. But we know satan, God's enemy and our enemy, gained a temporary victory through the temptation plot that welcomed sin into mankind and the world. Hear me on this truth. The only authority satan can achieve is when we sin and partner with Him. The good report is that in spite of this sin our God is a covenant God and King who operates with a Father's heart and love. Therefore, He made a way once and for all for satan to be defeated and conquered.

CREATION RESPONDS TO JESUS

Jesus was the first man to walk the earth since Adam who had complete authority. His life, ministry, and actions while on earth totally show this to be true. The seas became calm at His word; the fig tree withered at His rebuke; He cast out demons, healed the sick, raised the dead. Not only did He rule, reign, and exhibit stewardship during His ministry, but even in His death creation bowed to the true King. The Gospel of Matthew gives the picture of the power encounter that took place at Jesus' triumphal sacrifice.

> And Jesus cried again with a loud voice and gave up His spirit. And at once the curtain of the sanctuary of the temple was torn in two from top to bottom; the earth shook and the rocks were split. The tombs were opened and many bodies of the saints who had fallen asleep in death were raised [to life]; and coming out of the tombs after His resurrection, they went into the holy city and appeared to many people. When the centurion and those who were with him keeping watch over Jesus observed the earthquake and all that was happening,

*they were terribly frightened and filled with awe, and said,
Truly this was God's Son!* (Matthew 27:50-54 AMPC)

Friends, creation dramatically responded to the establishment of the government of the Kingdom of God and the overthrow of satan's dominion.

When Jesus voluntarily and obediently gave up His Spirit, He called out in a loud voice. This portrays one who was still operating in strength. Usually those who are near death seem to find it difficult to speak, particularly as they release their last breaths. It seems hard to fathom, but Jesus did not release His Spirit in a weak fashion. He exclaimed with a mighty and surprisingly loud voice, signifying in the spirit realm and the heavenlies that it carried authoritative weight causing soundwaves to be broken. Perhaps this was an announcement not only to those who were witnessing His death but also to the spiritual realm of satan and his army of demons. This was a declaration that He had successfully completed the mission of redeeming mankind and creation through the cross.

REDEMPTION FOR ALL

The particular time of day and year that Jesus gave up His Spirit coincided with the annual sacrifice of the Passover lamb as the priests made atonement for the sins of the Jews. At that moment, Jesus became the ultimate sacrifice making a way for repentance for the sins of all mankind. The veil in the temple was rent in two from top to bottom making a new way for all people—Jew and Gentile, male or female, free man or slave—to enter into the Lord's presence through a personal relationship with Jesus. No longer were animal sacrifices necessary or required because Jesus' was the perfect sacrifice given once for all.

The temple itself was divided into various courts—the Holy of Holies, the Holy Place, the priest's court, Israel's court, and courts for women and Gentiles. A dividing wall, approximately three or four feet high, ran through the Temple area separating the Court of the Gentiles from the inner court into which only the Jews were permitted. No longer was man's relationship with God dependent on trying to fulfill the Law as determined by the Jewish religious leaders. No longer was there any separation based on one's sex, race, ethnicity, or political status of those who desired to worship the true King.

RESURRECTION POWER

The power of death was defeated once and for all at the death and resurrection of Jesus. One of the miraculous signs was the opening of the tombs with many bodies of dead saints raised from the dead and appearing in the city. Can you imagine the response of those in the city to whom they appeared? It must have been a frightening and awesome experience to witness the power of death being completely defeated.

Many state that the tombs were opened as a result of the earthquake, which is a probable explanation. That being said, earthquakes do not hold resurrection power. I find it interesting that the Greek word *anoigo* means "to open," and it refers to God as the one who does the opening (Strong's #G455). And *egeiro* is the word used for "to be raised, to wake up, arouse or rise from the dead" (Strong's #G1453). When the power of death was defeated by Jesus, the ground could not hold the dead. The power of death over the land was broken and saints came forth just as this also serves as the prophetic sign that the redeemed will be raised and with Him.

THE EARTH SHOOK AND ROCKS SPLIT

It becomes more exciting as we continue to study this magnificent and holy moment. Scripture also explains that the earth shook and rocks split. This term for *earth* means the entire earth, all of the land. This was not exclusive to Golgotha or even Jerusalem. The entire creation shook. Obviously, this was a supernatural, intense reaction in response to the blood of our Savior being spilled on the land.

Genesis 4:10 tells us that when Cain killed Abel, the blood of Abel cried out to the Lord from the ground. This Scripture is stating that Abel's blood cried out for vengeance and justice at the sinful, evil act of Cain in his murder of his brother. You see, when the righteous are killed, the blood spills on the land and cries out for justice. This was the first instance of blood defiling the land; throughout Scripture we read that death, violence, idolatry, adultery, sexual immorality, and broken covenants, among other sins, also defile the land and creation. (In *Authority to Tread* I explain in depth the open doors that lead to defilement of the land and how to strategically cleanse the land and break the dark powers of these entry points.)

However, the blood of Jesus, speaking better things, cries out from the land that justice has been done and our sins forgiven. Jesus' blood speaks of forgiveness and restoration. On a personal level, we understand that the blood of Jesus cleanses, heals, protects, sets free, forgives, releases, and breaks the power of death and satan. It is through the shedding of His blood, death on the cross, and resurrection that we are redeemed. But the Lord came not only to redeem us and defeat the schemes of satan in our lives, but also to reclaim, restore, and reestablish His rule, His Kingdom, His government in the earth. As His blood spilled down and saturated the earth and He gave up His Spirit, His blood not only redeemed, healed, delivered, and transformed us, it also did the same for the physical creation. It is now our Lord's blood that has penetrated through satan's defilement to corrupt the earth. And it resounds out, echoing forever from the land in a holy cry for the souls of man and all of creation. "It is finished!"

The Greek word for shook is *seio*. It is translated "to shake, tremble, quake, move in the earth, or cause a cosmic disturbance" (Strong's #G4579). This word is normally used to signify God's wrath and judgment. In the scene of the crucifixion we might think of the earthquake as a demonstration of God's judgment against those who killed Jesus. But there is another meaning as well. *Seio* also signifies an emotional disturbance through fear, the stirring up or agitation of a crowd, and the upsetting of governmental affairs. The entire earth and the vastness of the heavens shook as our Savior died and His blood flowed down into the land. In this shaking was the tearing down, stripping, and disarming of satan's government over creation and the reestablishment of the government of the Kingdom of God.

The Greek word for split is *schizo*. It means "to break, chop, cleave, divide, open, rend, separate, split, and tear" (Strong's #G4977). The rocks split in response to the shaking of the earthquake, but they also split in response to the breaking and tearing down of the power satan had instituted in the Garden. The old covenant was fulfilled, and the new covenant of Jesus as the Rock of revelation upon which the Church, the Ekklesia, stands was established. When a power confrontation in the spiritual realm occurs and defilement is broken off the land, satan and his army of darkness lose their hold and the land and all of creation responds.

HE HAS CITIES, LANDS, AND NATIONS ON HIS HEART

Yes, Jesus engaged in this cosmic battle, but how does this apply to us? The Lord is concerned about the cities that we live in. Land is mentioned over 2,004 times in the Word of God. It is obviously a matter close to His heart. As outlined in Romans 8:18-21, creation waits with eager expectation for the revealing of the sons of God.

> *For I consider [from the standpoint of faith] that the sufferings of the present life are not worthy to be compared with the glory that is about to be revealed to us and in us! For [even the whole] creation [all nature] waits eagerly for the children of God to be revealed. For the creation was subjected to frustration and futility, not willingly [because of some intentional fault on its part], but by the will of Him who subjected it, in hope that the creation itself will*

also be freed from its bondage to decay [and gain entrance]
into the glorious freedom of the children of God (AMP).

Creation is meant to be partakers of the glory and the glorious freedom of the children of God. The phrase *earnest expectation* comes from the Greek word *apokaradokia* (Strong's #G603). This word actually is made up of three separate words. *Apo* is interpreted as "away"; *kara* means "the head"; *dokiem* means "to watch." Combined together, the words describe a vivid prophetic picture of a head erect and outstretched as if watching. They suggest a suspense in this waiting, like a watchman awaiting a beacon or signal to announce a victory in battle.

The Greek word for moaning is *sustenazo* and for pains of labor is *sunodino* (Strong's #G4959, G4944). The two words placed together signify that the whole creation is united in travail for deliverance from its bondage. The whole world of nature yearns for liberation from the agony of the ages, trembling in birth pangs and awaiting deliverance. It is not the cry of anguish as in the throes of death, but of birth and life. Just as a woman in labor has the hope and expectancy of birthing her child, so creation also travails in hope and expectancy. The word *creation* here refers to all of God's creation below human level that has been held captive to corruption. It is called to receive the blessing of deliverance, freedom, and redemption. The good news is mankind is the first fruit of the transformation and blessings that the Spirit has produced in the lives of those redeemed through Jesus. As first fruits and His blood appropriators, we can influence this earth. What we orchestrate, creation plays as a well-rehearsed orchestra under the guidance of a renowned conductor. If creation can resound with melody in the midst of enslavement and corruption due to man's sinful stewardship, then it can also play a newly composed piece of freedom and fruitfulness when we take our rightful places.

Now Is the Time

You see, the systems and structures of mankind are temporal and fading, but His is the Kingdom, the power, and the glory forever. We are not assigned to bring earth to heaven but to bring heaven to earth—the eternal Kingdom filled with glory. It is a now time to bring the glory of the eternal Kingdom to the sphere that is our Kingdom inheritance. It is a now time to see creation set free from sin, corruption, and decay. Some might be feeling that the world systems are too corrupt, too far gone for any level of breakthrough to be realized or for creation to respond to intercessory assignments. But I am here to tell you that corrupt systems and the earth can and will respond. How do I know? Because His written word declares it will be so. Rees Howells was mentioned previously in Chapter One, but allow me to share further testimony here.

Rees Howells led a dynamic group of 120 to 150 prayer warriors during World War II. They literally shaped history; they contended against one of the most horrific anti-Christ structures in the history of mankind—the Nazi regime. They faithfully carried their prayer assignment until the destruction of that system was realized. Even when the Nazis targeted Swansea, the city in Wales that was home to the Bible college and the prayer chapel founded and used by Rees and his intercessors, the bombs never touched the land or property of the school. They prayed on call no matter what time of day the Lord invited them as the prayer warriors and prophetic watchmen to sound their appeal. During this time, the Lord spoke very specifically of what was to unfold in the nations of the world concerning Hitler and the Nazi regime. This revelation came from deep intercession in the heights of the glory in the throne room and presence of Jesus. Rees and his faithful prayer warriors ascended higher to go deeper. Positioning and posturing themselves to be the vessels through whom the Holy Spirit prayed. It was years of devoted strategic intercession anointed in the glory realm full of prophetic revelation, prophetic decrees, binding principalities, and standing on the wall until that breakthrough came. Five years of abandoned, nonstop intercession. The intercession was not self-focused, nor was it solely focused on loving Jesus more. Hear me—this is absolutely good and right. However, the caution then becomes crossing over into a "bless me" mentality. To be honest, if this pattern lingers too long it halts all revival and transformation or any large-scale Kingdom transformation movement. The love and igniting in the revival empowers us to be effective in our warfare assignments. Nor was the intercession a one-time ascension into the throne room. It was fiery intercession contending against and pushing back an anti-Christ structure attempting to rule and reign in the earth realm. And friend, they triumphed. The victory the Lord assured them came to pass.

At the writing of this book, I have had the privilege of being in Wales and praying in the chapel at the Bible college where Rees and these warriors shaped history. Both times I have visited have been at the clear direction of the Lord to intercede in the glory realm anointing that was created on this land from years of being immersed in throne room intercession. One gentleman who was a part of the intercession is still living; he prayed with Rees' son and successor, Samuel. He passionately told Greg and I, "Rees and Samuel would adamantly say that there are three intercessors—Jesus, who makes intercession in His throne room; the Holy Spirit, who speaks and prays the prayer burden through each of us; and the intercessor and prayer warrior."

I greatly appreciate the wisdom of a dear friend in the persecuted church in Russia who one time explained, "There are two types of believers—those who only want the blessing of the Lord and seek only what they can get or those who receive the blessing of the Lord and take it out to transform society." Intercession at its core, including warfare prayer, is about giving of yourself on behalf of others, situations, cities, nations. It is not about what I can get; it is about what I can give. Intercession is a life of laying down for others. I must partner with the plans of the Lord to see schemes of the enemy defeated, a harvest come forth, and supernatural transformation realized. Intercession is a place of carrying the Lord's heart and passion for this lost world. It is a privileged place to hear His voice and to know Him. It is often a hidden place. Many may never know the hours spent before Him in that glory realm nor all the covert stealth assignments carried out in the land. But His glory will go before and behind you, and the reports of tangible breakthrough will be seen and known. No wonder the enemy is so busy trying to shut away the voice of the Church and to keep such wicked sin and violence in the nations. Where are those who will say it is more valuable to go beyond the personal benefits of our Christian faith and who resolve to go all the way, 100 percent sold out, releasing the glory He has placed in us to see the world turned upside down for His Kingdom?

It is my prayer that you hear what I am about to say. Strategic intercession to transform people, lands, and culture will not occur in one prayer meeting, one large gathering, or one three-day conference, although these gatherings are absolutely vital. Prophetically, I agree we are in a season of acceleration. There is power and authority in corporate gatherings. I travel our nation and the world speaking, prophesying, and interceding at such events and will most assuredly continue to do so. These corporate moments are an absolute necessity and serve as the converging point, a demarcation of synergy in His glory. They provide a venue to understand the season we are in, hearing the Lord in how to advance, receiving the tools and strategies to advance, and corporately decreeing His Word. It is then necessary for each of us to take those deposits back to our respective homes, cities, regions, and nations to implement that which was imparted. The leaders on the platform are not just called to be the glory carriers; we are all called to carry His glory. It is time we learn how to take our gates of influence, our *metron*, to see people, cities, lands, and regions freed.

CHAPTER SEVEN

WEAPONS TO INVADE REALMS

For though we walk in the flesh [as mortal men], we are not carrying on our [spiritual] warfare according to the flesh and using the weapons of man. The weapons of our warfare are not physical [weapons of flesh and blood]. Our weapons are divinely powerful for the destruction of fortresses. We are destroying sophisticated arguments and every exalted and proud thing that sets itself up against the [true] knowledge of God, and we are taking every thought and purpose captive to the obedience of Christ, being ready to punish every act of disobedience, when your own obedience [as a church] is complete.

—2 CORINTHIANS 10:3-6 AMP

Worldly weapons are not adequate to pulling down satan's strongholds. Things such as human ingenuity, talents, wealth, organizational skills, eloquence, propaganda, charisma, and personality will not aid us to victory in destroying schemes of the enemy. We cannot meet the world's challenges through humanistic thinking, psychology, exciting attractions, and performance. This also applies within the walls of the church as well. Worldly weapons cannot bring about a Holy Spirit awakening. Only the Spirit of God is able to bring a true move of God. If we look to the world's methods and are more concerned about cultural relevance, tragically the Church itself will be overwhelmed by the powers of darkness and its families thrown down and taken captive by the world's forces and satan and his army of darkness.

In order to see the schemes of darkness defeated and transformation realized, first and foremost we must know our battle is not against flesh and blood but principalities, powers, rulers of darkness, and spiritual hosts in the heavenly places. Oftentimes in the Church we aim our weapons at one another instead of the real enemy waging the battle against the Kingdom of God. Let's look at some of the more conventional and also not-so-explored or spoken-of weapons the Lord has given us to ensure breakthrough and victory.

THE ARMOR OF GOD

The most common teaching we hear when messages are delivered about weapons of warfare is Ephesians 6:14-17. During this time Paul was in a coupling chain bound to a Roman soldier 24 hours a day. Paul had ample time to study this Roman soldier and the armor that represented his warrior status. It is not farfetched to see how Paul might ponder the armor of this soldier while the Lord spoke to him about a better armor that we as believers are clothed in. We are to be girded with the belt of truth around our waist. It is Jesus and His truth that leads to life. We put on the breastplate of righteousness. So our hearts are protected by the holiness of the cleansing of our hands and purifying of our hearts. The shield of faith protects from satan's fiery darts. The helmet of salvation reminds us that we belong to Jesus and that we are assured of the final victory in battle. And no matter what circumstances surround us, we stand on a firm foundation of His peace.

But I would like to share a little bit of a different viewpoint on the armor. The armor is not just for our defense, but for offense. For too long, we as believers have stood and maneuvered in the armor from defense mode. We react to the enemy and his schemes after the assaults have been unleashed instead of using the weapons and our armor on the offense. Why do I say this? The sword is a powerful and significant weapon. It is absolutely used in defense and protection when an enemy is aggressively charging the armed soldier. But the sword is also used in offense when the armed one advances into battle. Many want to believe that since Jesus defeated satan on the cross, all we are expected to do is stand. A belief has developed that if we stand around with our hands in our pockets, evil will somehow not bother us or our society. But this is not what Paul was trying to convey. The word used for "stand" in this Scripture is an active tense. Standing does not mean we are stagnant and do nothing; it is an action stance we are to take to overcome the strongman and advance the Kingdom of God. Spiritual warfare is not just a defensive act; it is an offensive action and stance that obtains victory.

Joshua was on offense when he led the children to possess the Promised Land. Yes, God's enemies had stolen that land, but when they returned to possess it, Joshua did not wait to be attacked by his enemies. He received blueprint plans from the Lord for every battle and led the army of Israel in victorious offensive strikes to take their rightful Kingdom inheritance. Listen to this powerful challenge Joshua issued to the children of Israel to call them into order to advance: "How long will you put off entering to take possession of the land which the Lord, the God of your fathers, has given you?" (Josh. 18:3 AMP). To stand is an offensive position to engage and possess. What are other weapons to aid in the victory?

The Roar of the Lion of Judah

As I have been studying the fullness of what the filling of the Holy Spirit means for each of us, I have previously stated the Lord highlighted the day the Holy Spirit fell at Pentecost: "Suddenly, a sound like a mighty rushing wind came from heaven." In this portion of our study I want to look at this word *sound*. The translation of this word is "blast of the trumpet, good report, roar like the waves of the ocean, and to roar like a lion" (Strong's #G2279). Why is it so important to understand this word *sound*? Because when the Holy Spirit came on the day of Pentecost and filled the 120 in the Upper Room as discussed in Chapter Two, He went to the innermost part of a person that could respond to Him and transformed each of them from the inside out. That same Spirit, the breath of life of God, also carries a distinct transformational sound. It is a sound that speaks forth truth; it resounds like a trumpet. This roar of the lion is likened to the roar of the Lion of Judah. That sound and authority of His roar is imparted and deposited into each of us.

What are the implications of this? There is a sound within each of us that when we release it out into the spiritual atmosphere in agreement with Him, great authority resounds out; it shifts spiritual atmospheres and breaks barriers of darkness. As so strongly stated in Revelation 5:5, "Then one of the [twenty-four] elders said to me, 'Stop weeping! Look closely, the Lion of the tribe of Judah, the Root of David, has overcome and conquered! He can open the scroll and [break] its seven seals'" (AMP). Wow and yes! The Lion of the Tribe of Judah, the Root of David, has overcome and conquered. I am not saying authority comes with shouting and screaming at the enemy at the top of our lungs. But I am saying that what you speak out, prophesy, and what you release in Spirit in truth through praise and worship carries a distinct Kingdom authoritative sound that shifts atmospheres and breaks strongholds.

If the word *conquered* stretches your comfort zone, allow me to share further explanation concerning a Scripture previously highlighted, "When He had disarmed the rulers and authorities [those supernatural forces of evil operating against us], He made a public example of them [exhibiting them as captives in His triumphal procession], having triumphed over them through the cross" (Col. 2:15 AMP).

The phrase *public spectacle* refers to the victory parade of a conquering caesar king who, in returning to the capital after a great military victory, would publicly display on a victory march the spoils and prisoners of war before a cheering and adoring citizenry. It's a striking image of military conquest and victory. But subversively, the writer of Colossians suggests that on the cross Jesus is leading such a victory parade.

THE SOUND OF THE ROAR

When we read the Word, sometimes we distance ourselves from the magnitude of what it is trying to convey. I would like to share about an up-close and personal encounter I experienced with a lion several years ago that etched into my whole being the authority, magnitude, and importance of sound.

I had been invited to be a team member and speaker on a ministry trip to Zimbabwe. It was a powerful time of teaching, prophesying, and speaking into this nation at such a tumultuous time in its history. To make this trip even more special, there were Christian NBA players and Harlem Globetrotters who joined us on this mission. Their assignment was to go into schools and to teach basketball camps followed by a Gospel presentation giving the students and faculty an opportunity to be saved.

A gentleman who owned an animal refuge attended the large conference at which we all ministered that week. As a gift to the team, he offered to give us a free and private tour of this rescue center. Now, most of the animals had been rescued as babies and cubs. Please keep in mind that animals in Africa are really large. Many we saw that day had grown into their full adult selves. It was evident that they had been raised domestically even though in their grown (intimidating) size they had to live in habitats to be accommodated. The first habitat we visited was the one of Mr. Rhino. As we approached, he instantly recognized the owner and ran enthusiastically to the really large, strong wood fence (which, I might add, we were very thankful for). I have to admit, it was a little intimidating to have a rhino run full steam toward you. Although it was quickly apparent that he acted more like a huge puppy. He lowered his head over the top of the wood fence and began to pucker his lips to give the owner a kiss, which was gladly obliged. The owner then asked, "Don't you want to kiss those pretty ladies?" Mr. Rhino then turned his head toward us puckering his lips. I am just saying, ew! There was no way we were kissing Mr. Rhino that day.

We then made our way to the lion's habitat. That day they were in separate enclosures, one for the lioness and another for the lion. The lioness had the same response as Mr. Rhino. She made her way to the impressively tall and sturdy chain link fence. To be honest, it was like a chain link fence on steroids, for which, again, we were very grateful. Upon arrival, she began to rub her head on the fence much like a sweet little kitty, tilting it to the side wanting to be scratched behind the ear, all the while purring in contentment. So now we were all very eager for the opportunity to scratch behind her ear and to capture a picture of this rare moment.

It was now time to visit the lion habitat. All I can say is praise God again for the chain link fence on steroids! Mr. Lion followed the same pattern we had previously seen modeled by the lioness and rhino. But friends, when a grown lion walks toward the fence you are standing at and wants his ear to be scratched, his intimidating stance and stature definitely provide opportunity for an "overcoming" moment. He was big and stocky with very large and impressive fangs and claws. And yet he was majestic, regal, and royal. Within a few seconds we conquered our fears and eagerly awaited our turn to scratch Mr. Lion behind his ear—who, by the way, was contentedly purring. We were pleasantly surprised, and in our eyes Mr. Lion was now just a really big, friendly kitty.

Unknown to us, this whole scene was a set up. While we all pressed into the fence to scratch Mr. Lion behind the ear, the refuge owner had one of the workers deliver Mr. Lion's lunch. We were so fascinated at this unique occasion we had no clue what was transpiring inches away. Mr. Lion's lunch was contained in a deep bucket. It consisted of a significant sized piece of fresh red meat dripping with blood. Mischievously taking the opportunity of our fascinated distraction, that owner picked up that piece of fresh red meat and suddenly shoved it in front of Mr. Lion's nostrils and mouth.

Well, all I can say is abruptly Mr. Lion went from nice, purring kitty-kitty to an all-out king-of-the-jungle majestic roar. This occurred with the team standing only inches away, face to face with this mighty animal. Oh my goodness! It was a mighty roar, a mighty sound that penetrated every inch of our beings. All of the women froze in utter fear, our breath totally sucked out into the atmosphere with our lives flashing before our eyes. Those towering NBA stars, those championship winners, instantly screamed loudly at the top of their lungs like twelve-year-old girls and in unison ran! No hesitation or second thoughts over abandoning the women to fend for ourselves. I have never seen grown men scream in such fear and run so fast. What I would have given to capture our reactions on video. No doubt it would go viral across the nations of the world.

Even as I type the encounter, I find myself laughing out loud. It is a humorous story! But why I am sharing it with you? Because there is a sound. A sound of majesty, power, and authority in the roar of a lion that will strike fear and awe within every inch of your being. The lion is the king, he is majestic, he carries undeniable, tangible authority. He rules in his kingdom and domain. The same is true with Jesus, our majestic King, the Lion of the Tribe of Judah. When we praise, resound, and speak out in agreement with Jesus, we are of His tribe and His Kingdom. We carry and release a sound and authority of His glory and Kingdom. Let the Lion of Judah roar in our lives, families, cities, nation, and nations!

INVADING REALMS THROUGH SOUND: THE GOD OF GLORY THUNDERS

The voice of the Lord echoes through the skies and seas. The Glory-God reigns as he thunders in the clouds. So powerful is his voice, so brilliant and bright, how majestic as he thunders over the great waters! His tympanic thunder topples the strongest of trees. His symphonic sound splinters the mighty forests. Now he moves Zion's mountains by the might of his voice, shaking the snowy peaks with his earsplitting sound! The lightning-fire flashes, striking as he speaks. God reveals himself when he makes the fault lines quake, shaking deserts, speaking his voice. God's mighty voice makes the deer to give birth. His thunderbolt voice lays the forest bare. In his temple all fall before him with each one shouting, "Glory, glory, the God of glory!" Above the furious flood, the Enthroned One reigns, the King-God rules with eternity at his side. This is the one who gives his strength and might to his people. This is the Lord giving us his kiss of peace (Psalm 29:3-11 TPT).

Jesus has a roar and a voice. As descriptively written by David in this psalm, the Lord's voice is majestic, bright, and brilliant. His sound echoes through the skies. When He speaks, things happen. Actually, this is known as one of the loveliest poems ever written. It is pure and unrestrained praise. The name Yahweh (Jehovah) is found eighteen times in eleven verses. It is evident that David was a prophetic seer, and this psalm can properly be interpreted to speak of God's majesty revealed in the last days.

To help us gain further insight, the sea (great waters) is a term often used in the Bible to symbolize the sea of humanity. Trees in the Bible are symbols sometimes used for men. The strongest men are toppled and bowed down when the Glory-God speaks. The voice of the Lord is used seven times (the seven thunders) in this psalm. It is interesting that in Jewish synagogues this psalm is read on the first day of the feast of Pentecost. The Christian church was born on Pentecost two thousand years ago when the mighty rushing wind and storm of the Spirit came into the upper room as shared previously. The last word of this psalm is *peace*. It begins with a storm, but God brings His people peace even in the midst of storms.

THE LIGHTNING STRIKE OF SOUND

What is even more astounding is what occurs when you and I partner with Him. Allow me to share further insight from Isaiah 60:1: *"Arise, shine, for your light has come."* The meaning of this word *light* gives a great visual of what occurs when we speak forth in the anointing of agreement with His voice. One of the meanings of *light* is likened to lightning—that which is contrasted to darkness, enlightened judgment, the destructive light that precedes thunder, or, more pointedly, the voice of the Lord that thunders!

The following is a prophetic word that was released on the CD *Songs of Worship and Holiness: The Psalmist Trilogy III* by Kent Henry. I realize it is an older prophetic revelation, but when Greg and I were in the prayer chapel at the Bible College of Wales where glory intercession had occurred for decades, the Lord prompted Greg to pull out the old trilogy series. As we worshiped, the glory came and this prophetic word released in this worship series paints an awesome picture of what I am attempting to explain above.

I had a vision as I was getting ready to pray:

> I saw lightning that was white. But it came like a warm thaw. And it wasn't like lightning in the sky, it was like liquid lightning. But it was white. And right now, what I see is it just flowing upon you right now. And I said, Lord, "I have never seen such a vision. I've never seen lightning flow like water."

And He said, "You tell My servants that I have seen the cry of their hearts. I've seen the dedication of their hearts. I've seen the purpose of their hearts. And you tell them that the power of My Spirit is flowing into them even now. And that there will be new dimensions." He said the reason He showed me the lightning like liquid was that there are going to be new dimensions of the anointing that you have never experienced before. That you cannot understand, even as I am speaking, because it has never manifested before. He says to be open to it because it's going to come out in different ways and a different form. The likes that you have never seen. It will be a flow. It will be so natural. And it's going to come out as a liquid. And He says, "This liquid is going to cause a mighty harvest. It's not a harvest that comes up, but that jumps up in power."

As you continue to seek Him, seek Him as the God of the unexpected. You will begin to understand and walk in this unexpected. And everything that you have done here before, all the anointing you have flowed in before, all of that has been in preparation for this new anointing. He says, "You will keep the basis and the foundation of the anointing that you already have, but this will bring it to a new level and a new layer. It will flow. Even as the lightning can be seen for miles around. And many times, you see the lightning and then you hear the sound of it. Many times, the anointing will flow and even after the anointing hits, and even after it has been manifested, the sound of that anointing and the awakening that it causes will be echoed throughout the land. It will echo again and again and again."

And the Lord says that the light, the intensity of the brightness of His Spirit, will be followed up by the powerful sound of heaven's voice. You will hear that voice. It will come and echo in the reaffirmation of what was seen. So there will be an echo. First the brilliance with this anointing and then there will be that echo. And the echo is like thunder. And that thunder is just as powerful. It will shake. It will cause rafters to shake. And it will cause foundations to shake. This type of anointing has not been seen in many generations. You have been seeking that which has not been seen in many generations. And now it will begin to flow in you.

"I will draw people of like hearts and like minds and anointing to do work together. And what will begin to happen is that I am doing a new thing. Be very neutral as far as what you do, and allow Me to make the right connections to put all the right pieces together." And He says, "I will do some unusual things, some unexpected things. Always be ready to listen to the still small voice of My Spirit."

HIS WORD

For we have the living Word of God, which is full of energy, and it pierces more sharply than a two-edged sword. It will even penetrate to the very core of our being where soul and spirit, bone and marrow meet! It interprets and reveals the true thoughts and secret motives of our hearts (Hebrews 4:12 TPT).

We hear and know there is power in His written Word and prophetic Word. Allow me to elaborate further. Our soul and spirit are the unseen parts of each of us that make us who we are; joint and bone marrow are the physical aspects of our existence. All of these parts combined form our humanity. Therefore, God's Word has the ability to uncover our hidden aspects and make them known. To paint a more visual picture of this scriptural promise, in my studies of this Scripture I discovered the Aramaic word for *full of energy* can be translated "all-effective." There is a hint here of the spinning sword of fire held by the angel guarding the way to the Tree of Life. To come eat its fruit, you must pass through the mighty sword of fire. The context implies we pass through this fire-sword on our way into the Holy of Holies. When the veil was split in two, the cherubim embroidered on the veil parted to allow every worshiper to enter into the unveiled presence of God. The two-edged sword implies a two-mouthed sword. God speaks His word, then we, in agreement, also speak His word and it becomes a two-mouthed sword carrying His fire to be all-effective!

Praise and Worship

Proclaim his majesty, all you mighty champions, you sons of Almighty God, giving all the glory and strength back to him! Be in awe before his majesty. Be in awe before such power and might! Come worship wonderful Yahweh, arrayed in all his splendor, bowing in worship as he appears in all his holy beauty. Give him the honor due his name. Worship him wearing the glory-garments of your holy, priestly calling! (Psalm 29:1-2 TPT)

Your voice is a powerful weapon of warfare. Praise Him, exalt Him, adore and worship Him. You can bring the glory into any place in the world by your voice. When you open your mouth to praise Him and exalt Him, you will begin to hear the sound of the glory as it will fill the room. Praise and worship are two of the most powerful weapons of warfare. Whether engaging personally, corporately, or on an assignment, the sound of your exaltation to Him fills the atmosphere and darkness flees. Draw near to

God and He will draw near to you. Draw near to God, resist the devil, and He will flee from you.

PROPHETIC PROCLAMATION

Prophetic proclamation is defined as a prophetic decree serving as an announcement or ruling given with the authority of a prophet:

> *But the Lord stood with me, and strengthened me, so that through me the proclamation might be fully accomplished, and that all the Gentiles might hear; and I was rescued out of the lion's mouth* (2 Timothy 4:17 NASB).

To be a prophetic people, we are not to give scripted prophetic prayers or answers to the warfare assignments we engage in but prophecies, declarations, and decrees that are born in His presence, from His heart. Every city, land, and nation has its own calling and destiny. Hear me—God is a creative God. In our human understanding we feel more comfortable with an exact model to follow for every location we intercede on behalf of. There is not one set model or one set prayer. In the glory, we see as Jesus sees and intercession is made from that anointed now word of the Lord for the assignment. It is important when engaging in warfare prayer to not get in the trap of praying rote prayers. To achieve breakthrough, pray His agenda anointed in the Spirit. And definitely avoid praying from a place of flesh.

Oftentimes when we carry His assignments we realize God's true heart and intention is different from our opinion about a region, concluded in our own thoughts, mind, and flesh. If a region has wounded you, it is imperative to get healed and to not pray for it from your woundedness. We must always be in a growth process of knowing His Word, discovering His heart and love, rooted on the foundation of His truth, learning His voice, and most importantly engaging in His blueprint agenda that ensures victory.

PROPHETIC ACT

A prophetic act is a thing or deed done with the power of a prophet—an action or decree that foreshadows. One scriptural example is Joshua 6:3-5:

> *You shall march around the city, all the men of war circling the city once. You shall do so for six days. Also seven priests shall carry seven trumpets of ram's horns before the ark; then on the seventh day you shall march around the city seven times, and the priests shall blow the trumpets. It shall be that when they make a long blast with the ram's horn, and when you hear the sound of the trumpet' all the people shall shout with a great shout; and the wall of the city will fall down flat, and the people will go up every man straight ahead* (NASB).

TESTIMONY BY LANCE WALLNAU

The following is a testimony written by my friend Lance Wallnau in regard to an experience he had years ago with Kim Clement. I believe it is a clear example of much of what is being unfolded in this chapter.

Lessons from Kim on Worship and Warfare

One night I was with Kim at a meeting in Detroit and watched as he sat at the piano. Kim was a rare combination of classic pianist and prophetic voice with an uncanny word of knowledge. He was playing furiously and on this night he seemed to sound like Chopin improvising a movie score for a battle scene. Little did I know that somewhere in the midst of this concert his body kept playing but his spirit man was ascending up through a demonic realm that was screaming with agitation and protest. They were filled with terror that a redeemed saint was driving through their dimensional wall.

When Kim broke past this realm he entered another dimension—a heavenly realm where he heard other languages that sounded to him like angels speaking in other tongues. We should remember that Paul said "though I speak with the tongues of men and of angels" implying there is an angelic language. When Kim came back into his body he finished up his prophetic concert quickly and turned the meeting over to someone to wrap up.

Seeing in the Spirit

What happened next was most unusual. He had ascended into a place where, upon his return, he could see everyone's spiritual condition superimposed over their natural man. Hard to explain, but I will try. He looked at people and could see almost a three-dimensional projection of some quality about them that amplified what was developing in them spiritually. For instance, on one person he saw large eyes, which spoke to him of great perception. On another the garb of a mystic or monk, implying some deep quality of spiritual depth. On another a wreath of thorns, which suggested to him they were giving in to a spirit of false martyrdom because of rejection (remember Jesus bore the thorns so you don't have to). He didn't want to speak so we quietly slipped off into a car. The snow had freshly fallen and the ride was remarkably quiet as the fresh blanket of white rolled under our tires. Suddenly Kim lurched away from the passenger door and yelled "What was that!? Something hit us!" We assured him that nothing had happened, as there were few cars on the road. For the first time both I and another member of our team exchanged worried looks as we wondered what was going on with our friend. We drove on another 10 minutes and were shocked by what we saw as we turned into our hotel.

Police lights whirled amidst broken glass as an ambulance was busy working to tend a wreck that had happened exactly when Kim heard it and thought our car was hit—10 minutes earlier!

As Kim had been in a very different state than we were accustomed to we gave him extra time to come join us for our traditional late night debrief in the hotel. When he came downstairs he told us what he experienced and marveled that he was able to play the piano while seemingly being on a spiritual journey. (Remember Paul saying, "Whether in the body or out of the body only God knows"?)

I asked him if God showed him anything about himself and he said, "Yes, I was hardly expecting anything but as I went to splash water on my face I looked and my features were altered. I had a large jawline and had to look twice." I suggested that this was because he was, at that season in particular, demonstrating the voice of the Lord and serving as a prototype of the Last Days prophetic community Joel describes as a company of young "sons and daughters" who prophecy and elder folks who dream supernatural dreams.

Invading Realms Through Worship

It is interesting to me that this whole transaction took place while Kim was ministering to the Lord in worship. ... As Kim talked to us about the realm of second heaven, we explored further the area of spiritual resistance and demonic occupation. It seemed as if these spirits were shouting and shrieking that someone was invading their domain. They love to invade earth undetected but hate having traffic driven through their own courts.

Message to Warriors

Understand that the higher up you go on the Mountain of the Lord, the closer you get to your assignment on earth. The closer you get to your assignment, the closer you get to invading that second heaven realm of demonic resistance. Your job is to show up at the Gates of Influence in your assigned sphere. It does not matter that you are not well known on earth at these gates. What matters is that you are well known in heaven. When that happens you will be respected in the gates. Remember what the demonized man said to the unauthorized exorcists? You would expect them to know who Jesus was, but they knew Paul also, saying: "Jesus I know, and *Paul I know*; but who are you?" (Acts 19:15 NKJV).

IN CLOSING

Friends, I believe that praise and worship enveloped in prophetic intercession that is birthed in the glory is about to go to another level for the pure in heart. There is a sound that comes from the glory. It is a sound that is anointed and birthed in the glory. There is a price of faithfulness to be paid to get that anointing and sound. We will see in God's realms and as a result see others and situations with God's eyes in a way we've never seen before. It is the hour for the seers, hearers, intercessors, and believers to receive revelation that will empower us to have greater effect in our spheres and assignments. God intends to take His people into the realm where we penetrate the power structures of darkness and breakthrough occurs. And each of us, you and I, become God's lightning strike before the voice of the Lord that thunders! We are His legislative ambassadors as though He was making His appeal through us. And we become His empowered prophetic voice for defeating darkness and invading gates of influence to see His Kingdom come!

KEYS OF AUTHORITY

*Then I will set on his shoulder the key of the
house of David; when he opens no one will
shut, when he shuts no one will open.*
—Isaiah 22:22 AMP

We have weapons to invade realms! However, you might be pondering if contending against principalities is an off-limits activity for the church. What does Jesus tell us about our position of authority? As stated before, He has not left us to battle alone. He has given each of us keys. He has given each of us the authority to bind and loose. In Matthew 16:13-17, we have the historic core confession of the Body of Christ. It is Simon Peter's proclamation that Jesus is the Christ, the Son of the living God.

Now when Jesus went into the region of Caesarea Philippi, He asked His disciples, Who do people say that the Son of Man is? And they answered, Some say John the Baptist; others say

*Elijah; and others Jeremiah or one of the prophets. He said
to them, But who do you [yourselves] say that I am? Simon
Peter replied, You are the Christ, the Son of the living God.
Then Jesus answered him, Blessed (happy, fortunate, and to
be envied) are you, Simon Bar-Jonah. For flesh and blood
[men] have not revealed this to you, but My Father Who is in
heaven* (Matthew 16:13-17 AMPC).

Jesus then made a paradigm-shifting proclamation of His own to
Simon Peter: "And I tell you, you are Peter [Greek, *Petros*—a large piece
of rock], and on this rock [Greek, *petra*—a huge rock like Gibraltar] I will
build My church..." (Matt. 16:18 AMPC). Simon Peter, the first to make
this Kingdom declaration, was the first to receive the promise that God
would use him like a substantial piece of rock to build upon. Jesus stated
that joining Peter would be other believers who would also proclaim this
truth and represent the Kingdom of God. Together this Body would make
up a great rock, like Gibraltar—*petra*. And on this rock He would build
His Church, which I am now going to term *ekklesia*.

WHAT IS THE MEANING OF EKKLESIA?

The translation for the word *Church* in the above Scripture does not
portray what Jesus was powerfully stating. The literal meaning is "called-
out ones" or "assembly." The word is used 114 times in the New Testament,
and in 90 of these references a local church assembly is in view. However,
in this first use of *ekklesia*, it seems likely that Jesus had a more significant
and larger picture in mind. He was not just building a local assembly but
a worldwide Body of believers composed of all who make the same confession of faith that Peter made.

That being said, the word and concept of *ekklesia* was not new to the
disciples. It carried significant cultural emphasis. In this time of history,
this word was applied to the popular assembly of Greek citizens who helped

to govern a city or district (see Acts 19:32,39,41). Also, the Greek translation of the Old Testament used *ekklesia* to describe the congregation of Israel when it was corporately gathered when Moses presented the law in order for all of Israel to perform and carry out the law as a people and a culture.

In Greek and Roman society, the ekklesia consisted of ones who functioned in their cities as a senate or legislative governors in the land. They were known as a military task force of the culture they represented to cause things to appear as Greek or Roman. Their function carried with it the ideology to disciple people, cities, and nations. Why do we need to know this to be effective intercessors? To understand our keys of authority to bind and loose, we must realize the history-making message Jesus was relaying at this crucial moment. Allow me to explain further how history, misplaced translations, and words have shaped our effectiveness as the Church and as prayer warriors.

The Greek word *kyriakon* is the origin of the word *church* that we use in English. *Kyraikon* is composed of two words—*kyrias,* meaning the Lord, and *oikas,* meaning house or building. Combined together the meaning is clear—house of God or building. It is a purely religious word that originally meant temple or chapel, a physical location where people gather. It conveys something very different from the original meaning of ekklesia.

Historically and theologically it is a known fact that when the King James Bible was written in 1611 there was considerable argument over how this word *ekklesia* would be translated. The Tyndale translation done in 1525 accurately portrayed *ekklesia* as a governing body. By 1611 King James was head of the Anglican Church. The favored meaning of the word *church* under his leadership was that of a building. Therefore, this Greek word *kyraikon* was chosen as the basis for the English translation. Unfortunately, this word is not even in the Greek New Testament. This helps to give a clear picture why leaders have to keep explaining to people that church is not the building but rather the people of God who assemble to hear from Him, to be sent out, to pray and to release His Kingdom plans.

Further adding to the confusion, in AD 313 the emperor Constantine established himself as the head of the church controlled by the state and made Christianity the official religion of the Roman Empire. He began a massive building spree across the Roman Empire naming all the buildings after apostles from the Bible—for example, the church of St. Paul and the church of St. Peter. He declared himself the thirteenth apostle and erected statues of the twelve apostles in a massive building in Constantinople and included a much larger statue of himself in the building. He banned all house meetings and unofficial gatherings of any kind, and all had to gather in the buildings he had erected for their church services. Still to this day, all these years later, we think of the church as a building, not a Body of believers who pray and effect change. This in turn causes us to downsize the strategies of the enemy and our role to see victory obtained.

It Is Time for a New Paradigm

We see that immediately following His proclamation, Jesus focused on the position of authority in which the ekkleisa is to operate:

> *...and the gates of Hades (death) will not overpower it [by preventing the resurrection of the Christ]. I will give you the keys (authority) of the kingdom of heaven; and whatever you bind [forbid, declare to be improper and unlawful] on earth will have [already] been bound in heaven, and whatever you loose [permit, declare lawful] on earth will have [already] been loosed in heaven* (Matthew 16:18-19 AMP).

Gates of Hades

I believe Jesus was intentional about much of what He did. I find it interesting that when He initiated this discussion with the disciples He chose the location of Caesarea Philippi, home to Mount Hermon. It was known as the rock of the gods due to the many shrines that are carved into the face of the mountain. Shrines to Caesar, an open-air shrine to Pan and the court to the fertility goddess, Nemesis. It also houses a large cave called the gate of Hades. It was believed that baal-hermon would enter into the world from this cave. Worshipers would congregate and take part in bizarre, blatantly demonic sexual activities as well as rituals involving human and blood sacrifice. Jesus in a strategic move took His disciples to the most degenerate place possible. Clearly, He was making an object lesson.

The Lord of heaven and earth stands before His twelve disciples, and in a prophetic revelation of insight more vivid than the snow-capped glow of Mount Hermon—a place that fed the fears of men and demonically enticed surrender of their souls—Peter becomes the first human to acknowledge Jesus for who He really is. The King of kings and the Lord of lords. The Ancient of Days. Most Holy One. Lord of Hosts. Captain of the armies of God. The promised Messiah. Savior of the World. The Great I Am. Friends, when we get even a small glimpse into the complete kingship of our Savior, we stand at a new gateway or portal for understanding our own purpose on earth. Why? It is now known that Jesus not only possesses all authority, but that He also bestows it. Understanding this truth far better than His disciples, Jesus takes the opportunity in front of His chosen band of disciples to declare out loud that Hades will not prevail. As will be discussed in the testimony at the end of this chapter, unity is vital to breakthrough intercession. The size of the band of warriors is not the determining factor. Although, I will strongly emphasize here again that there are no lone rangers is dealing with principalities and territorial spirits. Individuals have been given authority over demons as stated clearly in Mark 16:17, "And these miracle signs will accompany those who believe: They will drive out demons in the power of my name" (TPT). But there needs to be a team or corporate assembly of the Ekklesia to defeat principalities. This can occur with a large governing assembly or even a band of warriors of two or three gathered together. What does matter is knowing God has assigned the battle—a clear revelation of the One who has directed you, a clarity of purpose that is voiced out in agreement among the gathered and convening Ekkelsia when on the land.

By standing at the rock of the gods, Jesus was making a clear and undeniable illustration. As the Church, we are His legislative body of people anointed in His glory to go to the darkest places of the world in order to destroy the schemes of the enemy and establish His Kingdom of light. One of the strongest demonic assignments and schemes of the enemy is the attempt to talk the church out of being the *Ekklesia*—the exact people to whom the glory of God has been imparted and distributed for stewarding and impacting the nations. It is not survival mode. It is overcoming and conquering mode. We carry governmental anointing in which our intercession made in partnership with the Lord can heal the past and shape the future.

Keys to the Kingdom

To understand fully what the Lord is saying about our Kingdom authority in this Scripture, it is necessary to explain a Jewish cultural understanding of the significance of handing over keys. In our modern, Western thinking, we would associate handing over keys as an act of granting someone full access to our home while they house sit or watch our home while we are out of town or on vacation. In Jewish culture, to hand over keys to one who is not the owner of the house meant they themselves were being entrusted with the full authority of that property—an authority equal to the master of that home. So what authority has been given to us?

"Behold, I give you the authority to trample on serpents and scorpions, and over all the power of the enemy, and nothing shall by any means hurt you" (Luke 10:19 NKJV). The Greek word for tread is *pateo,* meaning "to trample, crush with the feet, to advance by setting foot upon, tread upon, to encounter successfully the greatest perils from the machinations and persecutions with which satan would fain thwart the preaching of the Gospel" (Strong's #G3961).

Jesus Himself tells us that we have the au[...] and to defeat the schemes of the enemy. Ye[...] ture it is stated that the devil still has a measu[...] order for us, the Ekkelsia, to function in our full au[...] the difference between power and authority. satan has d[...] in the earth because Adam relinquished his birthright of d[...] power to him. However, he has never had kingly authority in th[...] Why? Because our heavenly Father kicked him and his rebellious army o[...] of heaven when their evil insurgency occurred, and in the temptation Jesus did not relinquish kingly authority to him. Satan might be the king of his dark army, but he is not the king of the earth because all of his attempts to gain full kingly authority were foiled and did not succeed. A kingdom is a legitimate institution with legitimate authority. To have dominion, domain, or power means you have to maintain it by force—which satan has maliciously attempted to do since the Fall.

But God! As shared before, Jesus as the King of kings defeated, stripped, and disarmed satan and his dark army on the cross and through His resurrection. He is now the One who possesses the keys and all authority associated with those keys. And friends, He has invested and bestowed to us, His Ekklesia, the highest conceivable authority. We are the keeper of the keys. We have the authority to tear down strongholds and to set the captives free. Authority always trumps power. But hear this word of wisdom—warfare prayer is not about flexing our spiritual muscles. Our joy comes from our identity in Him and that our names are written in the Lamb's book of life as stated in Luke 10:20: "However, do not rejoice that the spirits submit to you, but rejoice that your names are written in heaven" (NIV).

Binding and Loosing

To further develop our role in warfare prayer, the idea of binding and loosing was commonly taught by the rabbis. Binding was used to forbid, restrict, or prohibit. Loosing signifies to loose from ropes or straps, to untie

oing away with, and destroying something in order to permit and
. It is natural to see how these terms imply warfare language.

The disciples had already heard Jesus use the verb *to bind*. A
few chapters back, in Matthew 12. Jesus was talking about
warfare, namely, the conflict between the Kingdom of God
and the kingdom of satan. He then says to His disciples,
"How can one enter a strong man's house and plunder his
goods, unless he first binds the strong man? And then he will
plunder his house" (Matt. 12:29).

Jesus was carefully instructing His disciples about their
role in extending the Kingdom of God through invading the
kingdom of satan. Only the most naïve would imagine that
an aggressive assault on the kingdom of satan would be met
with anything but a desperate fight. That is why satan and
many of his principalities or powers attempting to stop the
spread of the Gospel must be bound. By whom? By the disciples of Jesus who are carrying the Good News to the lost.[1]

But hear my word of caution. We are not to engage in warfare pre-
sumptuously. I have been involved in warfare prayer and intercession for
many years. Warfare does not mean weird or flaky. Nor do we attack
everything we see as we have thoroughly discussed the vital role of knowing our assignment. We are given the authority to bind and loose. To
forbid and to permit. When our marching orders are from Him, He goes
before us and behind us. He sends His warring angels to attend to us and
to fight with us and for us. He gives us the ability to know the strategic
moment to move forward in the battle. Ecclesiastes 3:1 clearly explains
that, "There is a time for everything, and a season for every activity under
the heavens" (NIV).

RESTORATION OF ORIGINAL INTENT

The Church is in a season of invitation to become the full expression of the Kingdom of God, as was ordained at the foundation of creation—the original intent bestowed on Adam and Eve before the Fall. Satan has a migraine at the thought of this. The tensions we see manifesting in the earth are a sign of the times and a reaction to what God is doing. The enemy is being pushed into a corner because the glory is increasing. There is power in the name and blood of Jesus. At His name every knee will bow. At His name darkness trembles in utter fear. When Jesus and the Ekklesia show up on the scene, demons beg to maintain their territory and to not be driven out of regions. Why? Because Jesus is a demon tormentor. There is limitless power in His resurrection life. And we, the Church, are the fullness of Him who fills all and all. As declared in Ephesians 2:6, "He raised us up together with Him [when we believed], and seated us with Him in the heavenly *places*, [because we are] in Christ Jesus" (AMP). Why? It is from this place we are to bring heaven to earth. He has established a Kingdom of God culture that you and I and the world can step into.

> Then the seventh angel sounded [his trumpet]; and there were loud voices in heaven, saying, "The kingdom (dominion, rule) of the world has become the kingdom of our Lord and of His Christ; and He will reign forever and ever" (Revelation 11:15 AMP).

There is no equal between our heavenly Father and satan. The Kingdom of God envelops the kingdoms of the world and defeats and destroys the kingdom of darkness.

Jesus further states in Luke 11:20, "But if I cast out demons by the finger of God, then the kingdom of God has come upon you" (NASB). I will state it again—God and satan are not equal in their power or authority. Our heavenly Father, Jesus, and the Holy Spirit have more power in the pointing and waving of one finger than satan and his minions and all their power and authority combined. And when we are put on assignment by Him, this is the authority of which we are an heir and co-heir and for which the Ekklesia stands in the land and contends. It is in that place where breakthrough, victory, and transformation are realized. Allow me to share a modern-day example.

TRANSFORMATION IN PHILADELPHIA, MISSISSIPPI

In 2008, I was invited by Ruth Ann McDonald to teach on intercession. Upon my arrival, Ruth Ann shared the history of their small town, Philadelphia, Mississippi. Three civil rights workers—James Chaney, Andrew Goodman, and Michael Schwerner—had been hatefully murdered by the White Knights of the Ku Klux Klan on June 21, 1964. Justice was never duly served. Division, racism, and trauma had gripped the region. Ruth Ann and her small, powerful band of prayer warriors felt it was time for healing and breakthrough. On the same day of the week for two years, she and her prayer team stood on the murder site and prayed that Edgar Ray Killen, a Ku Klux Klan member and orchestrator of the murders, would be brought to justice. A series of events transpired causing the investigation to be reopened. On the fortieth anniversary of the murders, a cry of justice rose from the citizens of Mississippi. Edgar Ray Killen was arrested and indicted on January 6, 2005. On June 21, 2005, the forty-first anniversary of the murders, the 80-year-old Killen was found guilty of manslaughter and is currently serving three consecutive 20-year prison terms. It's amazing what can be accomplished through a few humble and obedient prayer warriors!

Ruth Ann voiced her appeal, "Teach us how we were able to see justice served. We need to understand strategic warfare more." Thus began the journey of me instructing and partnering with them in strategic warfare intercession.

Prior to my return in 2009, we continued to strategize and pray. From 2008 to 2009, much of the prayer was focused on the upcoming mayoral elections. On July 3, 2009, this town that had been steeped in racism experienced an amazing historic event. The first African American mayor was elected.

Ruth Ann also began sharing about the Choctaw nation and the strategic calling they carry to bring breakthrough and transformation. She felt strongly that I must meet a young Choctaw man, whom we will call John. Due to his marked sensitivity to the spirit realm, he had been chosen as a shaman. However, as the final rituals of his shaman training approached, Jesus appeared to him in a succession of three dreams that resulted in his salvation.

While ministering again in 2009, the Lord gave me a clear open vision. I saw two Choctaw men in a cave and what I would term a demonic principality of the queen of heaven descending between the two men. This demonic encounter resulted in division. At that point, I knew little about the history of the Choctaw. Per my request and the nudging of the Lord, we met with John. He confirmed what I was seeing and explained that in the Choctaw creation story they believe they were birthed out of the mouth of this cave shown to me in this vision. The head/source of the Pearl River is also situated at the mouth of this cave, which in turn runs into the Mississippi River.

He explained there were two brothers who had an intense disagreement in the cave, caused by this queen of heaven demonic being/principality. One brother left and took members of the tribe with him. This group became the Chickasaw. This gained my attention. Greg, my husband, is Chickasaw. I quickly understood that the Lord was entrusting us with a prayer strategy to deal with the root issue of racism and a covenant-breaking spirit.

When God is orchestrating a *kairos* Kingdom moment, He will ensure that all the necessary people are present to bring the transformational breakthrough. There were key intercessors and leaders attending the teaching that day. Representatives from the Choctaw and Chickasaw. An intercessor who had married into the family of one of the Klansmen involved in the killings of the civil rights workers. An African American pastor and those whose family members had been highly involved in free-masonry and the Ku Klux Klan. Every representative necessary to bring identificational repentance and healing to the racial covenant-breaking wounds of the region was at hand.

We strategized and drove to the cave. One key factor to include is that we ensured we had the welcome from the Choctaw to pray on their land. When we arrived it was night time. We were in the country surrounded by trees. Our cell phones had zero service. This was a problem. Greg was to join us by phone so he and John could initiate a time of identificational repentance. Having nothing to lose, I decided to dial our home number. Greg answered with a completely clear connection, "Hi, are you there and ready to pray?" We shrieked in amazement.

It was time for Greg and John to repent and establish covenant. Greg told us to go to the entrance of the cave. I hesitated and explained it was dark outside, that a pavilion had been built above the mouth of the cave and crawling under the pavilion was necessary to reach the entrance. He responded with a clear conviction, "Becca, you must to get to the mouth of that cave!" So, we got on our hands and knees and crawled to the entrance. Greg instructed us to put land in our hands, to pour anointing oil on top of the dirt, and to hold hands as an act of agreement. They repented Choctaw to Chickasaw and Chickasaw to Choctaw and established a new covenant as brothers with the land. I announced to that queen of heaven demonic territorial spirit that it was bound and its influence coming to an end. All division, racism, covenant breaking was ended. We prophetically called in the true apostles/prophets of the Choctaw and Chickasaw to arise and decreed that a move of God would be realized among the Choctaw in Phil-adelphia and Mississippi. We sounded the shofar and shouted a shout of breakthrough. Instantly, the call was dropped and I was unable to reach Greg again until we were two miles away from the cave.

John was greatly impacted and, upon returning home, shared with his aunt and mother all that occurred. The next morning, his aunt came to the church. I did not know who she was but felt a strong prompting of the Lord to give her a prophetic word. The Lord spoke the word "Chief." I was nervous to share this with her. Questions raced through my mind: "Do the Choctaw allow women to run for chief? Will she be open to hearing and receiving this prophetic word?"

I introduced myself to her and received permission to share the prophetic word I was hearing. "I know we do not know one another. But as I am praying for you, I keep hearing the word *Chief.* Are you thinking about running for Chief? If so, I feel the Lord is saying you are to do this."

She replied, "Your word is the confirmation I have been waiting for. My nephew is John and he came home last night explaining the miraculous time of prayer at the cave. The Lord told me that you are the prophet I have been waiting for to confirm I am to run and this is the reason I came today. If you released the prophetic word to run for Chief then I am to do it. So, yes, I am to run." As a promise, I told her Greg and I would return the week of the elections. (Just to make sure we are all on the same page— an elected Chief carries authority in leading their people, whichever Native American tribe that may be, much like the President of the United States does for a nation. They are a nation within a nation.)

Over the next two years, she and her campaign team worked tirelessly. She was running against a corrupt leader. Not only was there trouble through his decision-making process, but financially as a people they were struggling. Many were losing hope. To make matters more difficult, drought had greatly affected the region. She strongly desired better for their people. So on little money and a lot of faith in God, partnered with a strong belief in the power of prayer, they began the two-year campaign.

Greg and I kept our word and returned the week of the election. She stopped her campaign for one evening and served us dinner. She invited me to speak to her entire campaign team. The Lord led me to prophesy that she would win. That the journey to victory would seem impossible, but she would win the election and it would be the Choctaw moment in history.

Earlier that week, Ruth Ann was in the store and had an encounter with a shaman. He stated, "Whoever has the most power will win the election." Based on this encounter, we understood through clear guidance of the Lord that the elections would require further informed strategic warfare prayer to ensure our friend's victory.

The key location of this focused prayer was a burial mound. The day we prayed, it was over 100 degrees—miserably hot and no wind. As we worshipped, Sheila, Ruth Ann's worship leader, said, "It feels as if life is flowing through my feet." I told her to take her shoes off and to release life where there had been death and occult practices. When she did this prophetic act, a strong breeze blew across the fields and over the top of the mound. That breeze soon grew into an overpowering, intense wind making it difficult to stand. We all went to our knees to keep balanced. The temperature dropped drastically. Just as He had directed me to do at the cave two years prior, the Lord had me bind the queen of heaven principality. When I made this warfare decree a whirlwind came across the field and began circling the mound. Lightning began to flash. We were without words as it became visibly apparent that we had effectively broken the power of this spirit. We made our way to the car elated and awed by the moment we were witnessing. A deluge of rain began to fall. The drought had been broken. Since this time, the Mississippi River in many places had reached an all-time high in elevation.

On election night, June 14, 2011, a young Choctaw woman shared, "I had a vision of a white horse running across the Choctaw land. Redemption is about to happen." The results of the polls that night positioned our friend and the former Chief to enter into a runoff election. A month later she won the runoff, but the acting Chief refused to leave office. They went into a third election. Again, she won by more votes, and on September 6, 2011, the former Chief accepted his loss, announcing her as the first woman Chief. During this three-month timeframe, we continued to pray. Illegal money handling between Mercury Gaming and Titan Corporation had been exposed. Forty FBI agents converged on the casino and took all the hard drives and computers from the accounting offices. Since this time Mercury Gaming and Titan Corporation were also caught in illegal money handling in the state of Oklahoma and have been indicted.

October 4, 2011, was her historic inauguration day. The theme of her speech became the prophetic word spoken that night at the campaign headquarters, "Our Moment in History." There is great power and authority in an apostolic prophetic declaration from the highest governmental leader of a people group and nation. I believe we are seeing the fruit of this in Mississippi.

The Lord has led me to prophesy over Chief several times. One word was that she would become a key voice of Native Americans in Washington, D.C. She has made several trips to our nation's capital and carries great favor. Another word was that the Lord is entrusting her with seven keys to bring further wealth and prosperity to the Choctaw, Philadelphia, and Mississippi. She and her key staff and advisors pray through these spoken prophetic words, hear God's strategy, and do what He directs.

Chief has now completed her first term and was reelected for her second term in 2015. Here are a few things that have transpired under her leadership.

1. Bald eagles have now returned to Mississippi!

2. Business has greatly increased. Chief at one point had to request that the CEO of marketing of the restaurants, golf course, and recreational businesses pull back from some of the advertising until they can hire more

employees to keep up with the booming business in the hotels, resorts, concerts.

3. The Choctaw have built a hospital which is ranked as one of the top hospitals in that region. This has provided jobs and better healthcare.

4. They have built a new preschool providing more jobs and better education.

5. They are working on a transportation system from Jackson to Philadelphia that will financially benefit the state.

6. They are in the planning stages of tapping into the land and implementing an organic farm to provide healthy food and further employment.

7. From March 1, 2012 to March 1, 2013, the revenue in the Choctaw-owned businesses increased $3.7 million and continues to increase.

8. They are now ranked the number two employer in the state of Mississippi. At the time of writing this report, they employ over 6,000 people.

9. In May of 2013, Chief was awarded the Woman of the Year award in the political/state and government category by the Mississippi Commission on the Status of Women. She was chosen over two state lawmakers, the Senate secretary, and an eight-term mayor.

10. In February 2012, *Forbes* magazine wrote an article focusing on Chief. Below is an excerpt:

Under the astute leadership of Chief, the tribe continues to thrive and become a magnet for new industry and investors.

An innovative, forward-thinking approach to business has always been the tribe's practice. To further its economic success, the tribe is moving from traditional manufacturing into high technology pursuits. The tribe's outstanding progress in economic, educational and community development over the past 30 years not only attracts positive attention at home, but also at the state, regional, national and international levels.

By bringing people together and promoting unity, Chief is successfully leading the tribe out of the shadows of the national economic recession. She has been recognized as a visionary and consensus builder in Indian country and was selected by the White House to introduce U.S. President Barack Obama at the 3rd Annual White House Tribal Nations Conference, further demonstrating the respect she has earned from Indian and non-Indian leaders alike.[2]

Friends, when we enter into the God-ordained *kairos* strategic moment, that Issachar anointing for our regions, we can and do see supernatural, miraculous breakthrough.

IT IS TIME TO BE THE EKKLESIA!

The problem with being the church is nothing more or less than refusing to act like ekklesia. What do you do with a government that refuses to govern? In the United States, if our nation is suffering and failing do politicians' poll numbers go up? Of course not! Why? Because there is a direct connection between the prosperity of our land and the actions of our rulers. We voted them into a position of authority to actively solve problems. If they refuse to get involved, why are they there? Why are we seated with Christ on a throne, if we refuse to rule? Our passivity is actually rebellion, perhaps sedition, for it undermines His government. God forgive us! Ask yourself. Does death, sickness, poverty, gambling, alcoholism, child abuse, sex trafficking, drug lords or pornography have any legitimate voice or influence in Heaven? No, those are "already forbidden in heaven." As the ekklesia, we must start acting upon our charter. You have been given latitude to band together with others and rule in prayer. We are authorized and called to do so.[3]

You and I are the blood appropriators, spiritual legislators, the Kingdom of God governing senate to partner with the Lord in walking out this victory over darkness. You see, when we ascend into the heavenly glory realms, it expands us spiritually to receive His heart and His strategy for victory in war. This is exactly how Jesus operated and maneuvered. He did what He saw His Father doing and said what He heard the Father say. And friends, He is a creative God. Each time He calls you to advance His Kingdom, the blueprint strategy will be unique and different for each situation at hand. Do not attempt to put God or His ways in a box. We will see and learn His Kingdom principles and patterns, but it is so very key not to use our own human thinking to anticipate how He will move. His ways are above our ways. When we hear and receive the strategy from Him, He is anointing us to overcome into victory.

I will state it again—our job is to bring heaven on earth, to make the land look like heaven. What are we going to do about the problems that the world faces? Solutions for the world are found in the Ekklesia. It is our purpose as ambassadors of the Kingdom of God to be the standard-bearers in this world. Prayer is the cannon through which our spiritual warfare is aimed. The praying Ekklesia is the determining factor for what happens in nations. It is the prime place of leadership force to extend His Kingdom in order that "the earth shall be filled with the knowledge of the glory of God." History belongs to the intercessors.

ENGAGING PERSONAL VICTORY

*Father, I have manifested who you really are and I have
revealed you to the men and women that you gave to me.
They were yours, and you gave them to me, and they have
fastened your Word firmly to their hearts. And now at
last they know that everything I have is a gift from you.
And the very words you gave me to speak I have passed
on to them. They have received your words and carry
them in their hearts. They are convinced that I have come
from your presence, and they have fully believed that you
sent me to represent you. So with deep love, I pray for
my disciples....And I ask not only for these disciples, but
also for all those who will one day believe in me through
their message....For the very glory you have given to me
I have given them so that they will be joined together
as one and experience the same unity that we enjoy.*
—JOHN 17: 6-9,20,22, The Passion Translation

I love that Jesus opens this prayer by addressing our magnificent God as Father. He is Jesus' Father. He is our holy, heavenly Father. I am and always have been very much a daddy's girl. I loved my father, Ronnie Long, with all of my heart. He was a wonderful husband, father, and grandfather. He worked faithfully and honorably to ensure my mother and sister and I were taken care of and blessed. He was a father who instilled a belief that as long as we worked hard anything was possible to achieve. He was a great encourager, very patient, full of so much love and wisdom. He went to be with Jesus on January 21, 2008.

Even though I rejoice that he is in heaven, I still miss him greatly. It is always my heart to honor him and all that he worked for during his lifetime. As part of the normal proceedings after the passing of a loved one, we gathered for the official reading and legal recognition of my father's will. What if during this time a man whom we had never met entered that room? One we had no previous relationship with, yet he attempted to convince the judge that the inheritance my father worked so diligently to achieve was his. Obviously, none of us would sit by and allow this illegal squatter to rob our inheritance. The feisty warrior side of Becca Greenwood would most definitely rise up, and we would authoritatively command him to leave. If he persisted, we would have him physically removed and arrested. This illegal squatter would not be permitted to take the inheritance my father worked to ensure we had!

I believe all would agree with this stance. If we would do this so loyally and confidently in the natural, why would we not do the same in the spirit? As we have stated in previous chapters, the spirit realm is more real than the physical realm, and we must engage in such a way that the enemy is not able to rob us of the spiritual inheritance that our heavenly Father wants us to have and experience in our lives. To be warriors for the Kingdom of God, we must be diligent to seek Him and guard what has been entrusted to us.

PERSONAL FREEDOM IS OUR INHERITANCE

I also love that in the opening scripture of this chapter, Jesus inter-cedes and speaks forth a powerful and beautiful reality of the inheritance we have been blessed to receive, "And I ask not only for these disciples, but also for all those who will one day believe in me through their mes-sage....For the very glory you have given to me I have given them..." (John 17:20,22, TPT). Inheritance carries many implications. An *inheritance* is defined as a thing that is inherited, an endowment, provision, estate, birth-right, bestowal, portion, something that is or may be inherited, property passing at the owner's death to the heir or those entitled to succeed. From the beginning of creation our heavenly Father blessed Adam and Eve and all humankind with a rich inheritance. Genesis 1:26-28 explains:

> *God said, Let Us [Father, Son, and Holy Spirit] make mankind in Our image, after Our likeness, and let them have complete authority over the fish of the sea, the birds of the air, the [tame] beasts, and over all of the earth, and over everything that creeps upon the earth. So God created man in His own image, in the image and likeness of God He created him; male and female He created them. And God blessed them and said to them, Be fruitful, multiply, and fill the earth, and subdue it [using all its vast resources in the service of God and man]; and have dominion over the fish of the sea, the birds of the air, and over every living creature that moves upon the earth (AMPC).*

Our heavenly Father blessed man and woman with an inheritance and position of dominion. Dominion, *radah*, means to rule, tread upon, to have dominion, to manage, forceful authority, to trample, to reign (Strong's #H7287). The Hebrew word for bless is *barak* (Strong's #H1288). It means to speak words to invoke divine favor for a future time. It also means to bless God in adoration and that He blesses man, each of us, as a beneficiary. As previously discussed in Luke 10:19, Jesus spoke this truth concerning our inheritance in the realm of authority, "I give you authority to trample...over all the power of the enemy." As sons and daughters of our heavenly Father, we are to be a people of purpose and action of all that He has blessed us with as our Kingdom inheritance. And friends, that blessing carries granted and bestowed Kingdom authority.

Let's also look at this further scriptural promise:

> And these attesting signs will accompany those who believe: in My name they will drive out demons; they will speak in new languages; they will pick up serpents; and [even] if they drink anything deadly, it will not hurt them; they will lay their hands on the sick, and they will get well (Mark 16:17-18 AMPC).

I believe it is clear that in our Kingdom inheritance we are not to be shy but are called to be bold ones to exert this power and authority in our own lives, homes, cities, and regions. With this being our promised inheritance, then we must learn to apply these truths to our own lives as well.

HOW TO DEAL WITH THE GIANTS IN OUR OWN LIVES

One thing I always share concerning strategic warfare prayer is that we have to deal with the giants in our own lives before we deal with the giants in the land. As Paul clearly states in Second Corinthians 10:1-6:

> Now I, Paul, urge you by the gentleness and graciousness of Christ—I who am meek [so they say] when with you face to face, but bold [outspoken and fearless] toward you when absent! I ask that when I do come I will not be driven to the boldness that I intend to show toward those few who regard us as if we walked according to the flesh [like men without

the Spirit]. For though we walk in the flesh [as mortal men], we are not carrying on our [spiritual] warfare according to the flesh and using the weapons of man. The weapons of our warfare are not physical [weapons of flesh and blood]. Our weapons are divinely powerful for the destruction of fortresses. We are destroying sophisticated arguments and every exalted and proud thing that sets itself up against the [true] knowledge of God, and we are taking every thought and purpose captive to the obedience of Christ, being ready to punish every act of disobedience, when your own obedience [as a church] is complete (AMP).

I am not stating we have to be "perfect" to engage in battles for victory. However, it is imperative for us to deal with strongholds and sin patterns in our personal lives. I will term the level of warfare prayer being discussed in this chapter as *ground level*. It is what we all have commonly known as deliverance ministry or the practice of casting out demons. No human ingenuity, charisma, or ways of the world give us the ability, empowerment, or authority to defeat demonic strongholds. Only through the blood of Jesus, the name of Jesus, and anointing through the Holy Spirit will demons and satan flee. Not only do we want to deal with giants in our lives so we can experience personal freedom, but we also want freedom so our authority is not diminished as we contend against principalities and destroy fortresses, arguments, and every proud thing that exalts itself against the knowledge of God. Therefore, we must overcome fears, depression, rejection, sexual sin, unforgiveness, hurts, wounds, pride, unbelief, a religious spirit, etc. We must move beyond a wounded warrior status.

Let Him Complete the Deeper Work

To overcome giants in our lives, families, cities and regions, it will require seasons of personal growth and change. A time of coming before

Him to allow Him to do a deep, transforming work. I will share the promise of Second Corinthians 3:18 again:

> *Whenever, though, they turn to face God as Moses did, God removes the veil and there they are—face-to-face! They suddenly recognize that God is a living, personal presence, not a piece of chiseled stone. And when God is personally present, a living Spirit, that old, constricting legislation is recognized as obsolete. We're free of it! All of us! Nothing between us and God, our faces shining with the brightness of his face. And so we are transfigured much like the Messiah, our lives gradually becoming brighter and more beautiful as God enters our lives and we become like him* (MSG).

As we look into God's Word, encounter His presence, and see God's Son, the Spirit transforms us into the very image of God. We become alive and truly assured that we are free indeed. We engage in a visible change on the outside that is birthed on the inside. The awesome promise of God provided to us in this change? Moses *reflected* the glory of God, but you and I may *radiate* the glory of God. As glory carriers, one of our inherited promises is that we will carry His glory in our inner man. Where glory resides, darkness is confronted and must leave. Our lives becoming brighter and brighter and more beautiful like our Lord Jesus Christ as we grow "from glory to glory." Welcome the Holy Spirit to fill you with a transformational work. Allow these times of deeper work and change to come.

Out of the Overflow of the Heart the Mouth Speaks

The power of our words has already been discussed. Our mouths and tongues were meant to carry the fire of His truth. If our words are ones of death and not life, of rejection and not acceptance, anger and not peace, cursing and not blessing, then we are telling the enemy that he is doing a great job by our words, attention, focus. Who we spend the majority of our focus on will become the point or object of our worship. If we continually speak out what the enemy is doing, the fire of our words rests on his dark schemes, his plans are empowered, and he is now the focus and object of our worship. Our words are meant to carry fire, authority, and anointing to destroy the works of the enemy.

Identify Lies and Strongholds of the Mind

What we speak out is a strong indicator of where our thoughts and emotions are focused. A stronghold of the mind is a lie that satan has established in our thinking. It is a statement that we will count as true, but it is actually a false belief. In Second Corinthians 10:5, Paul describes strongholds of the mind as arguments. The Greek word is *logismous,* which is translated imaginations, arguments, or speculations (Strong's #G3053). It also means things that we will believe and count as true. The following are a few examples of a stronghold of the mind.

- I know I get too angry, but that is just how I am.

- I know pornography is wrong, but at least I am just watching the sexual sin and not actually sleeping with another person.

- I know I should not think critically about other people, but I know more than others.

- I know being married and attracted to another man is wrong, but I did not have sex with the man; I just kissed and touched him.

- I know the Bible states that sexual attraction to the same sex is sin, but the world tells me it is okay to be this way. I was born this way; therefore, I am going to embrace this homosexual lifestyle.

- I know things are really difficult in my marriage right now, but this happens to everyone and is just part of normal life.

- I want to be used by God, but I am not anointed enough. God really can't use me.

The reality is these lies will act as a shield of confusion and entrapment in our minds and thoughts to keep us from hearing the Lord, walking in freedom and victory, and advancing in strategic assignments to see breakthrough come. To receive further teaching on this topic you can read *Defeating Strongholds of the Mind*. It helps you to identify strongholds and also guides you in prayers to see them broken in your life. Once they are identified, it is a must to repent and renounce those lies.

Identify Strongmen in Your Life and Kick Them Out!

Not only do we need to identify strongholds in our thoughts but also identify and evict demonic strongmen from our lives. Jesus paid a high price to ensure your salvation and freedom from demonic strongholds. Be intentional to deal with generational curses, lifestyle choices, and ungodly forms of entertainment and sin. As we seek Him, He opens our spiritual eyes to see the assignments set against us and to see and hear how to break through that which has resisted us. And as one who has been set free from fear and depression, trust me, there is more power in one spoken word from our Savior than all the power of the enemy combined. When we hear His word of freedom decreed over us, demons flee in terror, we are free indeed, and atmospheres around us are transformed. Do not allow demonic spirits that are oppressing you to continue to keep their grip. Do not accept this as a part of your life. Submit yourself to a deliverance and inner healing ministry to break the enemy's grip in your life.

GUARD AND KEEP THE DEPOSIT ENTRUSTED TO YOU

O Timothy, guard and keep the deposit entrusted [to you]!
Turn away from the irreverent babble and godless chatter,

with the vain and empty and worldly phrases, and the subtle-ties and the contradictions in what is falsely called knowledge and spiritual illumination (1 Timothy 6:20 AMPC).

The Greek word for "guard" is *phylasso*. It carries different depths of meaning—to guard closely, to keep, watch, obey, guard during the watches of the night, to guard a people and a nation (Strong's #G5442). The Greek word for entrusted is *paratheken* (Strong's #G3872). It is that which has been entrusted to the care of someone, someone's responsibility to care for what has been committed unto them. Friends, the following is a key under-standing we all must have in the Body of Christ. To engage in personal victory, to begin to obtain to further measures of the authority that has been made available to us, we have to guard the beautiful treasures and gifts that have been freely given to us through Jesus and the Holy Spirit. We cannot live life void of the personal responsibility to cherish and guard the anointing, glory, and presence He bestows.

I find it interesting that one of the definitions of *guard* is to guard in the night watches. Many intercessors spend lengthy hours in worship, devotion, and glory-anointed, beyond-the-veil prophetic intercession in the night hours. While you might not be called to be with Him in the night hours, be faithful to be with Him when He calls. Allow Him to awaken your soul, and don't allow your hunger and passion to diminish or fall into slumber. Surrender and yield to Him. Let His presence increase in you to the place of anointing and from the place of anointing to abiding in His glory. Guard that which has been entrusted to you. Listen to the powerful words spoken from an anointed woman of God, Kathryn Kuhlman:

> The anointing...It costs much, but it is worth the cost. It costs everything. If you really want to know the price... You *really* want to know the price, I will tell you. It will cost you every-thing. Kathryn Kuhlman died a long time ago. I know the day, I know the hour. I can go to the spot...where Kathryn

Kuhlman died. But you see for me it was easy. Because I had nothing. One day I just looked up and said wonderful Jesus. I have nothing. I have nothing to give you but my love. That's all that I can give you is my love. And I give you my body as a living sacrifice. If you can take nothing and use it. Then here's nothing. Take it. It isn't silver vessels that He is asking for. It isn't golden vessels that He needs. He just needs yielded vessels.[1]

PURITY OF MOTIVES

If you've gotten anything at all out of following Christ, if his love has made any difference in your life, if being in a community of the Spirit means anything to you, if you have a heart, if you care— then do me a favor: Agree with each other, love each other, be deep-spirited friends. Don't push your way to the front; don't sweet-talk your way to the top. Put yourself aside, and help others get ahead. Don't be obsessed with getting your own advantage. Forget yourselves long enough to lend a helping hand (Philippians 2:3 MSG).

It is key to learn to prefer others better than yourself. Allow the Lord to do a work in your heart where you are not needing to be seen or heard for the sole purpose of validation. Seek Him to help you move in the motive that, in all you are doing, it is about His Kingdom being glorified. The anointing and the gifts He has imparted to you should not be about self-focused attention; rather, it should be on how it is used to draw men to Him, to extend the Kingdom, to see a harvest, to bring victory, breakthrough, and transformation. If we take the anointing and gift the Lord has given us and use it is solely for our benefit, then we become spiritually dry and in time will experience what I term spiritual anorexia. A pattern of prolonged, continual self-focus forces us into a dry and wilderness place.

Giving out is a Kingdom principle. You give out what He has given in the glory, and as you give out you fill back up in His presence and you give out more. Give what He has given you in order to grow and receive more.

Honor Unlocks the Glory

Honor our heavenly Father. Honor Jesus. Honor Holy Spirit. Be grateful for every person your life has touched and those who have touched your life. When honor is given it unlocks our heavenly Father's glory. What a beautiful world our honoring words and actions can create. Bless those who have gone before you and paved the way. Bless and honor those whom the Father has entrusted to you in your spiritual care. If you expect honor in your life then give it to others. Honor is not an entitled place, nor is it birthed from an entitlement attitude. Honor is not something that can be attained through force. Honor comes from a true heart of gratefulness and faithfulness. Honor even when your heart, mind, and emotions do not feel like honoring. It is an earned place in the spirit that shapes the attitudes of your heart. Honor unlocks the glory.

Don't Allow the Demonic to Rob Your Worship and Joy

How do we handle a demonic encounter? First, allow me to explain that if you are seeing in the Spirit, do not shrink back in fear. If dark spirits are invading your life, your dreams, your family, your home, you do not need to take this lying down. Address the spirits who are attempting to intimidate you and command them to go. The demonic should not be allowed to harass and intimidate. Stand on the truth that greater is He who is in us than he that is in the world. Second, if your mind and emotions are being attacked by the enemy, God gives us the ability to experience joy and to celebrate and praise in the midst of the battle.

As the Father loved Me, I also loved you. Remain in My love. If you keep My commandments, you will remain in My love, even as I have kept my Father's commandments and remain in His love. I have spoken these things to you, that My joy may remain in you, and that your joy may be full (John 15:9-11).

When we experience Jesus and His glory, we are filled with a faith that is stronger and bigger than our fears. Even when your emotions do not feel like it, open your mouth and worship our beautiful Savior. Worship Him, glorify Him. When we enter His presence with praise, He enters our circumstances with power, and the Lord shows us the way through the blockade.

When our minds and thoughts are racing in a wrong direction, one practice we have learned is to lay hands on our head and speak out loud, "I speak to my mind and my thoughts to come into alignment with the Spirit of God in me, my spirit man, the Word of God, and the truth of who He says I am as a daughter/son of the King. I welcome peace to my mind and my thoughts. Thank You, Lord, that You have given me power, love, and a sound mind." If it is an emotional issue, lay hands on your heart and speak out loud, "Holy Spirit, come and touch my emotions with Your love, peace, and joy. Holy Spirit, fill me up to overflowing with Your presence. I speak to my emotions to be filled with Him, His goodness and acceptance and love. Come into alignment with the Spirit of God. Emotions, we choose joy and peace today." Speak out loud scriptural promises of who He is and who He says you are as a son or daughter.

SHIFTING THE ATMOSPHERES IN OUR HOMES

To keep the atmosphere of His presence in your home, honor, love, peace, and prayer should be the culture. Reading the Bible together is so key. Welcome the sounds of worship to permeate the atmosphere of your home on a regular basis. And be the watchman and gatekeeper standing on guard on behalf of your family and home.

Allow me to paint a picture. My husband, Greg, and I have three beautiful daughters, Kendall, Rebecca, and Katie. We often tease that in order to get more testosterone in our home for Greg to not be so out-numbered by women, we bought one male dog, Buddy. Due to the fact that our home is filled with women, many times our family fun nights have involved watching episodes of shows such as "Say Yes to the Dress." Let's say for the sake of analogy that the Greenwood family is enjoying one such family night. Suddenly, a stranger bursts into our home, abruptly runs to one of our daughters, and begins to physically assault her. Are we going to ignore this intrusion and numbly turn the volume up on the television so we won't miss a moment of the show? Of course not! We are going to immediately rush to the aid of our daughter and will aggressively stop the assault in order to defend and protect her. I will ask this question again—if we will do this in the natural, why do we not do the same in the spirit? If we see spiritual attack and assault coming against our family, then we need to address it and deal with it. Do not give darkness permission to invade your space or your home.

EXPAND OUR MINDS INTO WHO HE SAYS WE ARE TO BE

Transforming our minds has already been mentioned, but I would like to state here that this transformation is not just the action of taking our thoughts captive. It is a growing and expanding of our thoughts and actions into who He says we are to be. I have a dear friend who is a great example of this truth. She is a pastor and in the past was a high school teacher. She began to receive prophetic words of being called to economy. She had no desire to be an economist nor had she ever received any training in this field. However, the word began to ring true in her spirit and she felt the Lord leading her in this direction. She allowed room for this to be birthed within her. She pulled herself aside in her prayer room with a leading book on economy open on her lap. She laid hands on her head and said, "Lord, if this is You, cause my mind to grow and expand into the anointing to fulfill this calling."

She welcomed the presence of the Lord into the process and she began to read that book. She said she had to read through the opening paragraph multiple times to even slightly comprehend the meaning of the words. As she continued to do this, she slowly began to understand the words on the pages and how economy is to function. In time, the Lord began to connect her with lead economists, and she, along with several others, has written a new economic structure based on Kingdom principles from the Holy Spirit prophetic revelation and Word of God. She now holds and leads economic summits and is speaking with certain government leaders in several nations about how they can implement the economic structure the Lord deposited in her mind and spirit.

MOVE BEYOND THE ME MENTALITY

Do not be fickle and inconsistent. Keep from a lifestyle of vacillating. Don't make the Kingdom journey you are on just about what is in it for you. While you do need to receive deliverance and freedom, do not get stuck in that place of always needing more deliverance and freedom. Get freedom and move on. I completely agree that we are all in process throughout our lives and always growing and being transformed into His image from glory to glory. This is great! However, I have witnessed the unfortunate cycle that many get stuck in. I will call this place *navel gazing*. It is the condition of always needing a healing or deliverance, a mindset of always being in an intense battle and never obtaining victory from the demonic strongmen that have gripped their lives. Or this trapped individual is always rehearsing past traumas to such an extent that they stay stuck in the pain. Their continual focus on the darkness and pain paralyzes them to move forward or to go beyond this inward focused place.

Do not get held in a rut. Do not always have your focus inward on yourself. Be so very grateful for what He has done for you and from that place go out and be an influencer for Him. Many times we obtain even more victory and freedom by helping and impacting others. "Because of this, brethren, be all the more solicitous and eager to make sure (to ratify, to strengthen, to make steadfast) your calling and election; for if you do this, you will never stumble or fall" (2 Pet. 1:10 AMPC).

Be Expectant

> Beware, in your prayers, above everything, of limiting God, not only by unbelief, but by imagining that you know what He can do. Expect unexpected things, above all that we ask or think.
>
> —ANDREW MURRAY, *The Ministry of Intercession*

Friends, it is time to stop being afraid of what can go wrong and get excited and expectant about what could go right. Put your hope, faith, and trust in Him that He can do exceedingly abundantly all that we ask or think. He is completely, fully, totally beyond measure able! Hear me. He does not want you bound and gripped by chains of darkness or schemes of the enemy that prevent you from freedom and victory.

Importance of Alignments

It is so very important to be with and glean from those who have gone before you and paved the way for the next generation. Be with those who see the calling and anointing in your life and who will pull that out of you. Be with those who have achieved freedom in their lives. Be with those who have paved a way in the areas you are called to and gifted in. Relationship and alignment is so very key. Find those who you know are your family or tribe. I cannot express enough how important it is in a season of overcoming to surround yourself with those whose faith can become your faith to press through into victory and breakthrough.

Be a Team Player

As discussed in Chapter Four, no battles are won without the work of a team. Scripture tells us, "For where two or three are assembled in My name, there I am in their midst" (Matt. 18:20). Jesus had a team of disciples. Paul traveled with a team and companions. David had an army, Deborah had an army, Gideon had an army. I could continue to list even more scriptural references. Having the mindset of a team player is a must.

Believe that He Is a Good Father

Rely on His love. Believe that He will *keep* you as the apple of His eye. That He covers you with His wings. Have your eyes, your gaze, and your mind on just one. Ensure that your purpose is fixed on Him. You can't manufacture this in your flesh. It is a Spirit-to-spirt work. Live for just one, the One who really matters. Live a life to please Him. Hear and know His voice. How can I speak with boldness and courage? From whom do I get my spiritual strength? From the One I love more than life itself. He is able. He is fighting for you and with you. He sends His angels to fight for you and on behalf of you. In spite of your mistakes or imperfections, allow Him to use you.

YOU WILL SEE OTHERS SET FREE AS YOU HAVE BEEN SET FREE

As I was radically set free from fear, depression, and outbursts of anger, I became passionate to see others set free. As a young mother of three, I remember being bound to the house with a daily routine of feedings, diaper changes, laundry, cooking, kissing little hurts, baths, cleaning and bedtime stories. Those years were precious, and I would not exchange one minute I had with my three beautiful daughters. Even so, I had a burning desire to know the Lord intimately and to see the lives of the hurting and lost transformed.

During that season of my life, I used the children's naptime for my times of prayer and intercession. The Lord began to place an intercessory burden on my heart for the lost mothers in our neighborhood. One thing I have learned as an intercessor is that the heartbeat of the Father is lost souls. There was one mother whom I began to pray for on a daily basis. And in the evenings Greg and I would prayer walk our neighborhood believing that those who were lost would be saved. God is so incredible! As we began to pray for her, she began inquiring about God and seeking counsel from me concerning issues in her home. Asking me to pray when difficult situations arose became a normal occurrence. The Lord was obviously drawing her to Himself.

One day the doorbell rang. I opened the door and there she stood. She asked if we could talk. I welcomed her instantly into our home. She told me that she and her husband were separated and that he was filing for divorce. I told her that I would begin praying that the Lord would restore their marriage. Her reply was, "I do not think that prayer and God can work through these hurts and wounds."

I responded, "No hurt or wound is too big for God. If He can create the universe in one spoken word. He can heal hurts, traumas and wounds in a marriage." I then prayed with her and asked the Lord to restore that marriage, to bring healing to all hurts and wounds, and to carry her family through that difficult time.

Over the next few months I prayed for her and her husband. Not only did I ask the Lord to restore their marriage, but I warred over their marriage and began to break every scheme and curse the enemy had placed on this couple. I prayed against division, unforgiveness, and every deception the enemy was perpetuating. In the name of Jesus, I broke the lie that this wound was too deep to be healed by God.

Soon our lives went in different directions. I took a part-time job and she took a full-time job. Even so, I continued to pray. One evening we passed each other driving through the neighborhood. She motioned for me to stop and roll down the car window. She then exclaimed, "Keep praying! It is working!" I gladly agreed and continued to pray. Two months later the children and I were swimming at the neighborhood pool. She and her children arrived at the pool and she approached me excitedly. "Your prayers have worked!" she exclaimed. "My husband returned home last week and he destroyed the divorce papers! God is good. Thank you for praying." I was thrilled. Not only did God restore the marriage, but this woman also began to attend church and to seek after the Lord.

Another few weeks passed. It was a leisurely Saturday afternoon as Greg and I were watching morning cartoons with our girls. There was a knock at the door. It was my neighbor with her whole brood of children. "Becca, do you believe in demons? That demons can torment a person and that they need to be set free?"

Obviously, this is not a normal question to be asked, so I calmly and cautiously answered, "Yes."

She exclaimed, "Oh good! As you know, we have been seeing the pastor of the church down the street for marriage counseling. I shared with him that I have a demon that comes into my room every night to intimidate me. That this has been occurring since childhood. I asked if he could get rid of it and make it leave. But he said that is not the type of counseling he does and suggested I contact someone who ministers deliverance to help with this issue. Becca, I thought of you. Can you help me?"

I gladly said, "Yes!" And while Greg and our girls and her children sat in our family room enjoying the morning show of Barney the dinosaur, I prayed for my neighbor in our master bedroom and she was totally set free from that demonic influence! It's just amazing what the Lord does and how He works!

POSSESSING YOUR
GATES OF INFLUENCE

Indeed I will greatly bless you, and I will greatly multiply
your descendants like the stars of the heavens and like
the sand on the seashore; and your seed shall possess
the gate of their enemies [as conquerors]. Through
your seed all the nations of the earth shall be blessed,
because you have heard and obeyed My voice.
—GENESIS 22:17-18 AMP

Cindy Jacobs shares a great truth concerning this Scripture:

> This powerful message was given to Abraham for his seed.
> We, the Church, are Abraham's spiritual seed and so this
> promise to possess the gates of the enemy pertains to us today.
> The gates of hell will not prevail against a praying Church.

Today's praying Church is rising up in militant force to possess the promised land of our nations.[1]

The Hebrew word for "possess" is *yaras*. It means to be an heir, to take as an inheritance, dispossess, drive out, conquer, take possession (Strong's #H3423). While some might feel uneasy with such strong language, allow me to give a brief overview of just a few in the Word of God who functioned in obedience and in some instances contended against demonic structures and, therefore, possessed spheres and gates.

- Joseph possessed administration and finance in a completely pagan culture.

- Abraham possessed nations of the earth.

- Deborah possessed city gates.

- Daniel possessed the government mountain of Israel's enemy.

- Esther persevered and possessed life, freedom, and victory for her people.

- David possessed a kingdom as a worshiper, warrior and king.

- Moses contended and delivered his people and possessed a nation.

- Joshua stayed in the tabernacle for 40 years, was anointed to take action, contended against the enemies of Yahweh, and possessed the Promised Land.

- Elijah contended against the prophets of baal and possessed victory.

- Jesus conquered satan and possessed all mankind and creation.

- Paul possessed cities, peoples, economies and regions.

- Peter possessed the lost, the Gentiles, and cities.

One practice all of these men and women observed was a faithful intercessory prayer life. Yes, we will all admit they had their flaws and weaknesses (except, of course, for Jesus). That was made clear in their life stories. However, their faithfulness to the Lord, His plans, and their devotion in prayer to Him was a constant theme throughout the history of these Kingdom of God history makers. The following is a powerful quote concerning intercession by E.M. Bounds.

> The more praying there is in the world the better the world will be, the mightier the forces against evil. ...God shapes the world by prayer. ...The prayers of God's saints are the capital stock in heaven by which Christ carries on His great work upon earth. ...God conditions the very life and prosperity of His cause on prayer. ..."You can do more than pray after you have prayed," said the godly Dr. A.J. Gordon, "but you cannot do more than pray until you have prayed."[2]

If these stated beliefs are true, which I fully believe they are, then prayer should and must be the uncompromising foundation empowering the business of our day.

It seems to me that each of these heroes of the faith had the mindset and understanding to obey, pray, contend, and possess. In my mind, this an awesome company to agree with and belong to!

GO THROUGH THE GATE AND LIFT UP A STANDARD

Isaiah 62:10 tells us to go through the gates. "Go through, go through the gates! Prepare the way for the people. Cast up, cast up the highway! Gather out the stones. Lift up a standard or ensign over and for the peoples" (AMPC). What does it mean to go through the gate? The Hebrew word for "gate" is *saar* (Strong's #H8179). It is the same word used in the Scripture of Genesis 22:17. It carries many meanings. I will share just a few. It is a large or smaller court area; a specific location where people would gather; a door that blocks the entrance of water; a place where people meet for market and where business is done; an area of the city where people meet for legal business; a city or population center, usually with a defensive wall and gate; a group of people who congregate at a gate; fellow townspeople. It is clear to see that the term *gate* signifies an important meaning concerning a city, a region, the marketplace, and legal business. Let's explore further. What does it mean to prepare the way, cast up the highway, to gather out the stones, and to lift up a standard over the people?

To prepare, *panah,* means to turn away or reject an object and to prepare, make ready, take actions of any kind to make an event or state possible (Strong's #H6437). A highway is a thoroughfare to physically get from one place to another. It emphasizes a journey of moving toward a destination, and usually it is a planned route. It also signifies conduct, meaning a way of life or what is done, such as behaving in a particular way with great importance on strength. When we are maneuvering in His strength there is vigor, might, power, or force greater than other entities. And through this strength we are to make ready, turn the way, and to cause circumstances to be prepared for some event.

I think we would agree that in all areas of society there are mindsets, ideologies, beliefs, and practices that are idolatrous in nature that hinder God's Kingdom from being extended. What is Isaiah indicating when he states to gather out the stones? The Hebrew word for "stone" is *eben*. It means a piece of rock; an instrument used for execution when thrown at a person in anger or justice, such as a slingstone; a stone slightly smaller than a fist, hurled at an enemy as a weapon (Strong's #H68). It also signifies a stone idol, meaning a piece of rock, fashioned or not, worshiped as an idol. The good news is this stone also represents a stone used as a building material.

Isaiah 62 goes on to tell us that we are to raise a standard, meaning to raise up, lift up, to have an object be at a higher elevation. As standard-bearers we are to have hands lifted high, ready to take a forceful action when there is a signal or request for help. And not only is there a calling to help but to also return to a safe position. Standard-bearers carry greatness, experience triumph, and walk in honor. They function in the stance of a warrior who is called to rise up in greater in power against their foe, but who also builds the new. When a standard is established it saves and delivers from danger or dire circumstances. As the standard-bearers we are to deliver, provide, and give whatever is necessary for the help and support of another to see an increase in volume. The prayer warrior reading this will appreciate that when we function as the glory-anointed standard-bearers we make a loud sound stronger than the softer sounds. The sound of the standard-bearer overpowers the sound of the flesh, the enemy, the world. There is strength in the sound of what we pray, prophesy, and decree.

You might be asking, "How does all this apply to me?" Friend, allow me to state again that you and I are called to go through gates of influence in order to prepare the way. Through His strength, power, and might we create the thoroughfare toward our desired destination. We remove all idols, building a new model by functioning as His glory standard-bearers to deliver and save from dire circumstances. We establish support to see an increase in lives, business, cities, nations. We are to possess gates of influence.

PROXIMITY IS POWER

Following a ten-day prayer meeting, the 120 in the Upper Room were in a united, close-proximity intercessory moment where all participants were anointed with the baptism of the fire of the Holy Spirit. As stated before, in that instant, instead of beholding the burning bush they became the burning bush. Each of them became a living torch full of the fire of the Holy Spirit, as described by Smith Wigglesworth:

When a child of God is filled with the Holy Ghost, the Spirit makes intercession through him or her for the saints according to the will of God. He fills us with longings and desires until we are in a place of fervency as of a molten fire.[3]

You see, this was not just for the 120. What they prayed and believed for was a breakthrough birthing moment that changed the world. The way was made for all believers to have the same anointing and authority. Think about how drastically the perception of the 120 changed at that moment. They shifted from hiding away from danger in the Upper Room to suddenly and boldly proclaiming the message of the Kingdom of God outside the walls of their corporate gathering place. They had experienced such an incredible paradigm shift, they came out of a personal focus into an emboldened and empowered Kingdom purpose.

That day, as Peter preached, 3,000 got saved. They began to impact every realm of society because they were filled with the Holy Spirit, anointed with great power, and encountering the glory of the Lord. They became apostles of great influence carrying the glory with them everywhere they went. They got outside of the walls, got in proximity to the gates of influence they were called to, and turned people, people groups, cities, and regions upside down for the Kingdom of God.

The Bible shares testimony throughout the Old Testament and New Testament of those who were in direct proximity to and contended against evil forces in the supernatural realm at gates of influence. The results were great, measurable, tangible victories. The significance of the Upper Room is that it was a ten-day prayer gathering that changed the face of Christianity for an eternity. This supernatural historic moment was not just for fire and glory, but also an empowerment to overthrow through authority and possess with supernatural boldness. To do so, proximity is key. Proximity means nearness in place, time, order, occurrence, or relation. In other words, proximity is power!

Proximity to Him

God wants us to be personally revived in His glory realm, not just to survive one day after the next. As we are revived, we are anointed and appointed to be ministers of reconciliation and transformation.

> *All this is from God, who through Christ reconciled us to himself and gave us the ministry of reconciliation; that is, in Christ God was reconciling the world to himself, not counting their trespasses against them, and entrusting to us the message of reconciliation. Therefore, we are ambassadors for Christ, God making his appeal through us. We implore you on behalf of Christ, be reconciled to God* (2 Corinthians 5:18-20 ESV).

To reconcile means we are to make things right. An ambassador is to represent or to be a ruling authority. This is not implying control or force, but we are to be ones who stand, pray, and contend to become His voice for salvation, change, breakthrough, and transformation. This means that the more time we spend with Him, the more we will receive His wisdom and creative strategy in the realms of culture and society that He has called us to and positioned us in. Do we spend enough time with Him to allow His creativity to bring us into new forms of favor and success? Are we dying to self and receiving more of Him in order that we increase in spiritual authority in the realms and spheres we engage on a daily basis? Do we know and hear His voice prophetically leading us?

Proximity in the Gate of Influence

We become glory carriers in order to take His Kingdom throughout society and culture. We have to be in proximity to Him and then in proximity of those we are called to influence. Meeting together as the Body of Christ is good. Corporate, united, close-proximity intercession times are a must. However, I believe these gatherings serve the purpose of preparing us to take His Kingdom and light into the world. If we want to influence and be world changers, we must be in proximity to and engaged in those areas

He has called us to. Glory-anointed intercession produces glory-anointed strategies where action steps are outlined to see His Kingdom come.

If we are going to contend in warfare to bring breakthrough to our gates of influence and the lands and regions we are called to, more times than not the glory presence and authority we have been given must be released in those spheres and on that land. Hear me. Authority to possess gates and have dominion is inextricably linked with personal responsibility to carry burdens and assignments through to the end. This applies to any area we are being called to, such as government, education, media, arts and entertainment, business, family, medicine, Church, neighborhoods, Bible study groups, cities, regions, nations. It is key to begin to step out in faith in the *kairos* strategic time and to take action steps toward the calling. How do you do this? Seek His leading and take the first baby step of obedience, then take the next step, and then the next. Begin to build relationships with those who can influence and mentor in the area of your passion and gifting.

Stand in the Gate of Influence

When He reveals breakthrough warfare assignments and Kingdom assignments, He will call us to intercede at and to be planted and building in the geographical location that is in need of healing, deliverance, and reconciliation. True transformation comes when we stand on the land, in the gate, and in the place God is calling us to redeem. We bring His presence, glory, anointing, and authority. We are spiritual atmosphere changers.

Get the Strategy from the Lord

John Wesley said, "God does nothing but in answer to prayer."[4] S.D. Gordon said, "The greatest thing anyone can do for God and for man is to pray. Prayer is striking the winning blow...Service is gathering up the results."[5] The truth is, our Father is a creative strategist and does not leave us to fight the battles alone. He will give us strategies of impact and breakthrough. Remember to stay in the position of the Holy Spirit speaking the strategy to you.

SHUT THE DEMONIC GATE

What is my point in sharing these truths? It is clear we are to be ones who conquer those demonic strongholds the enemy has set up to establish his standard in the realm of the hearts of men and spheres of influence. But not only are we to conquer schemes of darkness, we are to possess for the Lord. As we discussed deliverance and casting out demons in the last chapter, I want to highlight occult-level warfare in this chapter. Occult-level warfare is dealing with a more advanced structure of demonic activity. Warfare at this level usually deals with things such as witchcraft, Eastern religion, shamanism, occult secret societies, and satanism. *Occult* is defined as supernatural, mystical, or magical beliefs, practices, or phenomena that are hidden from view and done in secret. It is not the only type of warfare that is engaged in within our spheres of influence. Contending against principalities and territorial spirits will be discussed in the next chapter, but to gain insight of how to deal with this occult realm of warfare let's look at a scriptural example of one who conquered and possessed where it is clear that contending in this occult dimension was a part of the strategic action.

Moses: Let God's People Go

Many are familiar with the story of Moses and Aaron challenging Pharaoh to let God's people go. I would like to use this scriptural example because I find it extremely interesting that the Lord Himself gave Moses the lessons of how to engage in miraculous signs and wonders against the powers of divination utilized in Pharaoh's government. Moses had been in the wilderness and on the mountain with the burning bush and therefore had received an impartation from the fire presence of the Lord (see Exod. 3). You see, to have victory in the realm of warfare, especially occult warfare, we must have the earned authority that is gained by being in His holy, glorious presence. We must have the earned authority of ones who have been in the presence of His fire and walked through the fires and trails of life but have come out as overcomers set aflame with His heart, glory, passion, and authority. We must have earned authority that comes from acts of obedience. Not only had Moses been in the presence of the Lord, he had been in the Lord's school of learning the miraculous signs and wonders while on the mountain of the burning bush.

God Himself trained Moses in the strategies He would implement through him and Aaron to defeat the demonic structures of divination and sorcery operating through Pharaoh.

> *And Moses answered, But behold, they will not believe me or listen to and obey my voice; for they will say, The Lord has not appeared to you. And the Lord said to him, What is that in your hand? And he said, A rod. And He said, Cast it on the ground. And he did so and it became a serpent [the symbol of royal and divine power worn on the crown of the Pharaohs]; and Moses fled from before it. And the Lord said to Moses, Put forth your hand and take it by the tail. And he stretched out his hand and caught it, and it became a rod in his hand, [This you shall do, said the Lord] that the elders may believe that the Lord, the God of their fathers, of Abraham, of Isaac, and of Jacob, has indeed appeared to you* (Exodus 4:1-5 AMPC).

He taught Moses how to hear His voice, to respond in obedience, and to see and execute the signs and wonders necessary to contend against and defeat the structures holding back the children of Israel from the promise of deliverance and freedom. Here we see again that when our Father sends us into the assignment He will make the necessary provisions to see the victory come. Let's look at the encounter with Pharaoh in Exodus 7:8-12:

> *And the Lord said to Moses and Aaron, When Pharaoh says to you, Prove [your authority] by a miracle, then tell Aaron, Throw your rod down before Pharaoh, that it may become a serpent. So Moses and Aaron went to Pharaoh and did as*

the Lord had commanded; Aaron threw down his rod before Pharaoh and his servants, and it became a serpent. Then Pharaoh called for the wise men [skilled in magic and divination] and the sorcerers (wizards and jugglers). And they also, these magicians of Egypt, did similar things with their enchantments and secret arts. For they cast down every man his rod and they became serpents; but Aaron's rod swallowed up their rods" (AMPC).

It is interesting that Pharaoh would request for Moses and Aaron to prove their authority. Why would he do this? Because in occult practices the only true signs of the practitioners' authority and effectiveness are signs and wonders produced in the demonic realm. The priests were using supernatural demonic power, but God's power is always more powerful than anything satan can conjure in the spirit realm. While I realize Scripture tells us that the Lord hardened Pharaoh's heart, the Lord's strategy was to confront the occult sorcery and beliefs through His visible power and authority to defeat these demonic occult powers being performed through the priests. In occult realms of warfare, more times than not it requires a supernatural act of the Lord, a power encounter, to see dark structures and systems defeated. It is like a showdown in the spirit realm, but God always has the victory. We see the Lord using this pattern throughout the ten plagues that ultimately ended in the release of Israel.

OPEN THE PORTAL OF GLORY

Following the power confrontations of the ten plagues, Pharaoh agreed to release the children of Israel and they were delivered from bondage and set free. During their years in the wilderness, they were positioned to rebuild the tabernacle of the Lord, which was enveloped with the cloud of His glory by day and His fire by night. Joshua, Moses' successor, spent 40 years in the presence of the Lord in a tent of meeting. This produced an opened gate of glory that prepared Joshua and the next generation to conquer enemies and possess the land.

Possess Your Gates of Influence

Upon the death of Moses, the glory-anointed Joshua entered the Promised Land, battled their enemies, and victoriously defeated them. Here is the result of his obedience in contending in warfare, destroying the works of their enemy, and leading the children of Israel to victory:

> And the Lord gave to Israel all the land which He had sworn to give to their fathers, and they possessed it and dwelt in it. The Lord gave them rest round about, just as He had sworn to their fathers. Not one of all their enemies withstood them; the Lord delivered all their enemies into their hands. There failed no part of any good thing which the Lord had promised to the house of Israel; all came to pass (Joshua 21:43-45 AMPC).

I will reiterate here—to possess means to be an heir, to take as an inheritance, to dispossess, drive out, conquer, and take possession. The result of this strategy is rest and blessing in the land.

The Harpers' Testimony

Yes, we read about these victories in the Word of God, but what about now? Allow me to share the following testimony shared by my friends, the Harpers.

> Five generations of Harpers have mined in Arizona since the late 1800s. Today, our family owns an aggregate mining operation in the Gila River located west of greater Phoenix. As the aggregate producer we are the first link in the chain of products used to create the roads and freeways you drive on, every sidewalk and curb, the runways at airports, every commercial and government building from the mall to your

local schools and so much more. If you live in a home with a cement foundation, the aggregate producer played a significant part in building it.

In 2005, our mine was shut down, and we were forced into a legal battle that lasted five years. It was traumatic. An outright betrayal, and the most grievous of setbacks that never should have been. We found ourselves thrust into the most intense spiritual warfare of our lives. The recession that began in late 2007 dealt us yet another huge blow. The structure of the Arizona economy, highly tied to the construction industry, made Arizona one of the hardest hit states by the economic and financial crisis, after being ranked in the top two states from calendar year 2004 to 2006, second only to Nevada. For calendar year 2010, Arizona's national ranking had tumbled to 49 with Nevada at 50. Ultimately, God gave us the victory. In the eyes of the world, we won the lawsuit. But for years, I couldn't consider it a win. It cost us nearly everything to be right.

In the summer of 2010 we went back into the Gila River to start over in a very sluggish economy. Vandals and thieves had stolen all the copper wire out of everything, including our office, and most of the machinery was inoperable. The cost of starting over looked near impossible given our financial situation. We had been five years with no income. All our retirement funds and our children's college savings were gone. We had taken on a significant amount of debt to sustain. We looked the demon of insolvency in the face but refused to relent. We were exhausted from the fight; hanging on to God and our hope with all the strength we had left.

During those years, I earnestly sought an intimacy and a personal relationship with God, devouring His Word unlike any time in the past. I needed to lose the fear of whether God would continue to take care of us. I had to learn to redefine prosperity. The day I was no longer afraid was the day I became prosperous. He truly is the rewarder of those who diligently seek Him (see Heb. 11:6).

In the fall of 2013 I was invited to attend the Regional Transformation Spiritual Warfare School founded by Greg and Becca Greenwood and being taught by Deb Welch. In that class and others I was attending through Wagner Leadership Institute, I began learning about breakthrough. I gained fresh revelation that as believers wherever we go the Kingdom of God is made manifest. We carry with us the power to shift atmospheres! I also began to get a much deeper understanding of the principality we had been warring against!

I'm baffled by the sheer number of believers who attend church religiously week after week, year after year, listening for something they haven't heard, yet only seem to produce audiences and not armies. I was among them until strategic prayer made me a warrior. In strategic warfare prayer, prophetic insight and experience is combined with mapping, research, and the Word so that the land can be redeemed. Armies of believers are united to carry the very heart of God literally around the globe to every sphere of society, and perhaps most importantly to our own backyards. The understanding I gained about strategic prayer has been the most paradigm shifting lesson to impact life in my backyard— the marketplace.

Throughout the class, we pieced together information that revealed what principality we were dealing with on the land at our mine. There had been bloody wars, massacres, rain making cults, broken covenants, and 138 years of litigation over water rights taking place on the land within a one-mile radius of our mine. There is a significant monument from which every parcel of land in Arizona has been surveyed. This stretch of the Gila River had also been a dumping ground for dead bodies murdered in drug deals gone bad. The mine is also located at the confluence of three rivers—the Agua Fria, the Gila, and the Salt—that just happen to meet at the lowest lying spot in the Phoenix metropolitan area.

The most significant discovery was key facts about a form of the queen of heaven called Sophia. She is often referred to as "The Lady in the Lake" who is worshiped in many ways, but also occult practices. As we excavate aggregate, we dig very large, deep lakes. During our legal battle, our adversary had filed a plat map with the county requesting permits to build a housing development around the lakes that we had dug. He named it Lake Sophia. There is a day of feasts celebrated for Sophia every year on November 28. When I went back into our legal records, I discovered that we were shut down on Monday, November 28, 2005. We knew that date would be key for strategic prayer at the mine. November 28, 2013 was also a rare occurrence between the Hebrew calendar and the Gregorian calendar, making it the first time in 152 years that Thanksgiving Day and Hanukkah fell on the same day. We often say in our strategic prayer circles, "You just can't make this stuff up!"

After praying and breaking the hold of Sophia, we began to see significant breakthroughs within ten days! Family members and employees began experiencing God in new and fresh ways. A new start-up cement company operating on our property began seeing daily increases in jobs and quantities of cement sold. Five years later, that company is still growing, having more than doubled in size. Our once vacant corner is now occupied by a second tenant cement company. In the history of our business we have never had more than one cement company on site. For the first time in nine years, we started hiring more employees to keep up with demand!

As government goes so goes the economy and business. As strategic prayer armies have invested much time and effort praying for our nation and the state of Arizona governmentally, we've seen unprecedented favor with our governing authorities. We were the only aggregate producing mine among many applicants in the county that was issued a new mining permit in 2014. Today, we're seeing enormous impact in the rollback of regulations nationally and locally. We're also seeing significant impact in tax reform for small business nationally and locally. We've been able to pay off what looked like insurmountable debt in record time!

Through a miraculous turn of events that only God could orchestrate, we partnered with Christian, Kingdom-minded investors. That partnership allowed us to begin the process of opening our second mine location. In October 2017 that very prosperous start up cement company I mentioned purchased our original mine location. This sale allowed us to move our administrative offices to our west mine location, which now holds more minable resources than at any time in our family mining history. We're also seeing manufacturing return to the U.S.—this impact on our local economy is *big!*

A developer of hydrogen-powered big rigs announced its plans to build a $1 billion plant in Arizona. Construction of the manufacturing facility is scheduled to begin in 2019 bringing thousands of job opportunities to the West Valley. An investment firm recently paid $80 million to acquire

25,000 acres of land in the West Valley with plans to build a technologically integrated "smart" city from the ground up. Our new mine location is positioned beautifully to provide the material necessary to build the infrastructure for both projects. This mine will be producing aggregate material to build the foundations of communities for generations. As I write this we are planning our grand opening celebration for the west mine location where we will start monthly prayer meetings for business leaders to convene at our offices for worship and prayer.

We need God's help to restore optimism for the discouraged and opportunity for the downtrodden. We want to see God turn the economic growth today into prosperity that endures for generations. The potential impact of our prayer is as limitless as our *God!*

The hour I held our first meeting in the new office was the hour I realized my promised land and my destiny have converged! What a difference strategic prayer has made! My life will never be the same. The lives of our family, our employees, and their families—the lives of our business associates, lives directly connected to this industry, and the lives of those whose communities we build are forever changed! I will always be grateful to Deb and Jack Welch for inviting me to that strategic prayer class back in 2013.

GLORY IN THE LAND

If individuals can be born again, why can't cities,
made up of many individuals, be born again?
—C. Peter Wagner,
The Church in the Workplace

Jesus came to bring redemption to all mankind. He came to set us free. He came to set people groups free. He came to see demonic systems and structures defeated and destroyed. He came to see the land and creation set free and brought back into its original purpose. He came that we can stand with Him and for Him in gates of influence to see all spheres of culture set free. And He came to see cities, regions, lands, and nations healed and transformed.

> *When it goes well with the [uncompromisingly] righteous, the*
> *city rejoices, but when the wicked perish, there are shouts of*
> *joy. By the blessing of the influence of the upright and God's*

favor [because of them] the city is exalted, but it is overthrown by the mouth of the wicked (Proverbs 11:10-11 AMPC).

Ask of Me, and I will give You the nations as Your inheritance, and the uttermost parts of the earth as Your possession (Psalm 2:8 AMPC).

And My people, who are called by My Name, humble themselves, and pray and seek (crave, require as a necessity) My face and turn from their wicked ways, then I will hear [them] from heaven, and forgive their sin and heal their land (2 Chronicles 7:14 AMP).

Cities are exalted by the upright. He gives the nations and the ends of the earth as our possession and inheritance. If we will humble ourselves, seek His face, and turn from our wicked ways, He will hear from heaven, forgive our sins, and heal our land.

It is evident that God is in the business of forgiving, exalting cities, healing lands, and giving the nations and the uttermost parts of the earth as an inheritance. To see His Kingdom manifested and His glory in the lands in which we are positioned, oftentimes it will involve an engagement in prophetic intercession, prophetic decrees, and strategic warfare prayer. While these are not the only actions utilized to see transformation realized, it is often a key part of the process. What does this level of intercession involve? Allow me to state that I have been involved in this form of intercession for over twenty-six years but do not claim to have all the answers. I believe we are all in the process of learning and growing. That being said, in this chapter it is my goal to share the wisdom and revelation we have gained over the years and to stir a passion in each of you who are called to pray at this level.

If you will recall, in Chapter Two we discussed spiritual warfare being a power confrontation between the Kingdom of God and the kingdom of darkness. And it is clear that satan and his army of fallen angels are diligently scheming to establish his evil kingdom. How does he do this over cities, regions, and nations? Satan's dark representatives will position themselves at his command over geographic regions. They rule illegally, acting as illegal squatters. As these demonic entities take hold on the land and in the heavenlies they have a direct effect on the people living in those assigned territories. A door is opened for these dark angels to establish their demonic grip in regions through the acts of repeated sin and mis-stewardship of the land involving activities such as sexual immorality, broken covenants, bloodshed, idolatry, God-robbing. Not only does the enemy try to grip cites, lands, and regions, but as discussed in the last chapter he does so in all spheres of culture and gates of influence. The truth is most people are unaware of satan's devices and fall prey in some measure to the spiritual influence of these territorial spirits. Cindy Jacobs shares an eye-opening truth in *Possessing the Gates of the Enemy*:

> We are in a holy war for the souls of men and women. We are wrestling in heavenly places against an enemy who is ruthless in his desire to steal, kill and destroy. He is the master strategist who wants to pervert God's design for the nations. He has undermined the rule of the Kingdom of light and established his thrones and dominions. And one of his greatest weapons is passivity on the part of believers. While we have been busy in the churches he has been carefully instituting his rule in the nations of the world.[1]

These high-ranking spirits are identified in Ephesians 6:12, which we have already quoted in the book, but for the sake of the process I will reference it again: "For we wrestle not against flesh and blood, but against principalities, against powers, against the rulers of the darkness of this world, against spiritual wickedness in high places" (KJV). Prophetic strategic warfare prayer to heal cites, regions, and gates of influence involves power confrontations with high-ranking principalities and powers assigned to geographical territories and social networks. These entities are also referred to as master spirits or territorial spirits. Their assignment is to keep large numbers of humans—networked through cities, neighborhoods, regions, nations, people groups, industries, governments, businesses, education systems, religious alliances, media, or any other form of social institution—in spiritual captivity. Results of this oppression include but are not limited to the rampant injustice, oppression, misery, hunger, disease, natural disasters, racism, human trafficking, economic greed, wars, and the like now plaguing our world. Some might be wondering where we see these spirits mentioned in the Word of God.

Nebuchadnezzar was so influenced by the prince of Persia that he made a golden image of himself and commanded all to bow down and worship him as god. The prince of Persia also used Nebuchadnezzar as a pawn to force demonic worship. However, God broke the back of that principality when He displayed His magnificent glory in the fiery furnace as the fourth man in that raging fire. The light and authority of His glory dispelled satan's darkness.

The same demonic entity identified as the prince of Persia tried to kill Daniel. In this evil scheme he tricked Darius by the plot he had also used on Nebuchadnezzar by stirring up the governors of the kingdom and the administrators, counselors, and advisors. It appeared to be a dismal scene for Daniel. This dark prince had appeared to do his homework to know what would cause the demise of Daniel. But God rescued Daniel out of the lion's den and once again the power of the prince of Persia was broken for a season. For the sake of this study, let's delve a little deeper into a New Testament battle that was waged in the heavenlies and where victory was obtained.

EPHESUS: SAVING A CITY AND CORRUPT ECONOMIES

Magic was big business in Ephesus. Spells, charms, amulets, totems, statues to Artemis, and other demon gods and scrolls were used for just about everything. From blessing a business venture to the healing of diseases, witchcraft was called upon to provide the remedy. But as the Kingdom of God began to make an inroad into Ephesus, this occult business took a heavy blow!

The story is told in Acts 19. Some Jewish exorcists, seeing the power displayed by Paul, were invoking the name of Jesus in casting out demons. One day, the seven sons of Sceva, a Jewish high priest, were attempting to cast out a demon by invoking the names of Paul and Jesus. But that spirit exclaimed, "Jesus I know, and Paul I know; but who are you?" (Acts 19:15 NKJV). They were then assaulted by that demonized man and were severely beaten. No one wants a "seven sons of Sceva" experience in deliverance ministry or spiritual warfare assignments.

Word about this botched deliverance session got around town. Also, the power of Jesus over demons was becoming a clear reality. The result? Many Ephesians converted to Christianity and in doing so make a huge bonfire to burn all of their magic stuff!

Many who practiced magic brought their books together and burned them before everyone. They calculated their value, which equaled fifty thousand drachmas. So the word of the Lord powerfully grew and spread (Acts 19:19-20).

Friends, this is 50,000 silver coins going up in flames! Modern-day historians say this would be approximately the equivalent of over 7 million dollars. This was a million-dollar bonfire. And markets tend to notice this much money being torched. Sure enough, they did. The markets got spooked and anxious. And predictably, this spilled over into acts of violence.

About that time there arose a great disturbance about the Way. A silversmith named Demetrius, who made silver shrines of Artemis, brought in a lot of business for the craftsmen there. He called them together, along with the workers in related trades, and said: "You know, my friends, that we receive a good income from this business. And you see and hear how this fellow Paul has convinced and led astray large numbers of people here in Ephesus and in practically the whole province of Asia. He says that gods made by human hands are no gods at all. There is danger not only that our trade will lose its good name, but also that the temple of the great goddess Artemis will be discredited; and the goddess herself, who is worshiped throughout the province of Asia and the world, will be robbed of her divine majesty."

When they heard this, they were furious and began shouting: "Great is Artemis of the Ephesians!" Soon the whole city was in an uproar. The people seized Gaius and Aristarchus, Paul's traveling companions from Macedonia, and all of them rushed into the theater together (Acts 19:23-29 NIV).

I could go into an in-depth teaching here, but suffice it to say that this power confrontation against the demonic stronghold and principality of the region, a form of the queen of heaven named Artemis, carried great spiritual authority to set a region free and to impact the economy in the marketplace. When the Kingdom of God took authority, the bottom line of the spreadsheet was greatly affected. Salvation began to break out. Paul's authority over demons and principalities prompted a multi-million-dollar disruption in the magic trade, which in turn threatened the principality of Artemis, greatly affected the idol market, and the entire spiritual atmosphere of a city began to transform.

Here we see again the principle that proximity is power. When the Lord's anointed glory carriers arrive in a region and they move in supernatural signs and wonders, it sets the stage for a divinely orchestrated power confrontation against strongholds and His Kingdom begins to break open and break out. When the Kingdom of light comes in fullness it pushes darkness to the forefront. The enemy and his army will overplay their hand and expose themselves in an attempt to keep their hold, but God's

Kingdom prevails. His gates fling wide open and the King of Glory is ushered in. The gates of Hades shall not prevail against His Church, His glory-anointed and appointed Ekklesia.

WISDOM TO ENGAGE

As we discuss this form of intercession, one chapter does not suffice to enter into a full teaching on this topic. This type of intercession is not to be entered into lightly and there are steps of wisdom that can be gleaned and put into practice. I must honestly admit—being one who is specialized in tearing down strongholds over a region was not something I was searching to enter into. Oftentimes, I have pondered how one goes from singing opera and performing on the stage to prophesying into nations and engaging in intercession and warfare that involves tearing down strongholds. The only answer is God. I do feel that those who are gifted in prophecy and intercession and who have a call to cities, regions, and nations carry an authority to tear down strongholds. It is part of the anointing that these giftings bring. However, this is not to say that other believers cannot be trained in this. The word of wisdom is that it must be done with care, but at the same time expectancy.

DO NOT DESPISE THE JERUSALEM WHERE HE HAS CALLED YOU

For some this might not be an issue, but for me in a past season this was a condition in my heart that needed His healing touch. We had moved from Texas to Colorado Springs in the year 2000 to work for Peter and Doris Wagner and Chuck Pierce at Global Harvest Ministries. We were confident that this was the new season the Lord had for us. Before our move, several friends had cautioned me concerning the spiritual atmosphere of the city, explaining that it was not easy for those gifted in prophecy and intercession. However, in my unprepared thinking I would ponder how this could be true. After all there were over 120 Christian ministries thriving in the city and many key leaders made the city their ministry base.

Once we arrived, I soon realized that my friends were speaking truth. It is a beautiful city, but at that time it proved to be difficult to prophetically hear the Lord and to break through into His presence. As a worshiper, prophetic intercessor, and warrior, this was not an easy adjustment. I was also born and raised in Texas and had lived in this state my entire life prior to this move. I often tease that you can take the girl out of Texas, but you can't take Texas out of the girl. The atmosphere in Colorado proved very different. We were beyond honored to be with Peter, Doris, and Chuck. The job part of our move was wonderful, but I was struggling in the city. I began to inform the Lord that we had misunderstood Him by making this move and asked Him to open doors for us to return to Texas. I prayed this consistently for over five years. Not only was I attempting to sway the Lord to relocate us, but I regularly spoke about the difficulty of the city and with my mouth spoke negative words and curses out in the atmosphere.

It was 2007. I was speaking at a ladies' retreat in Vermont. In prayer the Lord led me to teach about possessing the land. I was already feeling this was a different topic to teach at a women's gathering but strongly felt the Lord leading this direction. That night the glory of the Lord fell in the meeting room. Everyone was either kneeling or lying prostrate on the floor. No one, including the worship leader, was standing. She was lying on her back on the platform, playing the guitar. His presence was so holy she did not want to stand.

As I lay prostrate on the floor I heard Him ask a question: "Becca, you are teaching these women about possessing their land."

I replied, "Yes, Lord, You led me to teach this, right?"

He gently spoke without hesitation, "Yes, I did, but how can you teach these women to possess their land if you despise the Jerusalem where I have placed you?"

Ouch! I will be very transparent. I began to weep, "Lord, please don't ask me to do this." But soon I was completely undone and did exactly what

He was asking of me: "Lord, please forgive me for despising where You have placed us and cursing the people and the land. Help me to love my city, the region, and the state with Your heart."

As soon as I prayed that prayer He took me in a vision. I was soaring with Him over the state of Colorado. He asked me, "Becca, do you see it, do you feel it, do you hear it?"

Why was He asking this? Because in this vision I could see, hear, and feel the winds of revival blowing across the plains of Colorado. I assuredly said, "Yes, I see it, I hear it, I feel it!"

He responded, "Then get up, go back, and be one to help make that happen."

Wow. Even typing this I am undone. While I am not certain we will live all of our days in this state, I can guarantee you that I now love the people, city, region, and state with His heart. I no longer curse the city in which I live but speak blessing to the people and land. Friends, if you want to have impact that transforms and brings His glory to the lands and nations He is leading you to, do not despise the Jerusalem where He has placed you, but love the people and the land with His heart. Pray, intercede, and contend from His heart and Kingdom perspective.

DEALING WITH GIANTS IN YOUR LIFE

We have discussed how to be an effective special ops prayer warrior and also how to move beyond being a wounded warrior. It is imperative to remember what we discussed in Chapter Nine and that we walk in deliverance and inner healing when engaging against principalities. We can't tear down what we ourselves might be holding up.

Move in His Timing

Joshua issued a powerful question to the children of Israel: "How long will you delay going out to take possession of the land that the Lord, the God of your fathers, gave you?" (Josh. 18:3 CSB). It is true that Joshua led the children of Israel to possess the land. However, due to their refusal to fight the giants, the children of Israel wandered in the wilderness for 40 years. Moses sent Joshua, Caleb, and the spies to see the situation of the Promised Land and its inhabitants. After 40 days they returned. Moses and Aaron gathered the children to hear the report.

> *"We went to the land to which you sent us and, oh! It does flow with milk and honey! Just look at this fruit! The only thing is that the people who live there are fierce, their cities are huge and well-fortified. Worse yet, we saw descendants of the giant Anak. Amalekites are spread out in the Negev; Hittites, Jebusites, and Amorites hold the hill country; and the Canaanites are established on the Mediterranean Sea and along the Jordan." Caleb interrupted, called for silence before Moses and said, "Let's go up and take the land—now. We can do it." But the others said, "We can't attack those people; they're way stronger than we are." They spread scary rumors among the People of Israel. They said, "We scouted out the land from one end to the other—it's a land that swallows people whole. Everybody we saw was huge. Why, we even saw the Nephilim giants (the Anak giants come from the Nephilim). Alongside them we felt like grasshoppers. And they looked down on us as if we were grasshoppers"* (Numbers 13:27-33 MSG).

As a result of their fear, the twisting of the truth, and a false report, they delayed the promise of God. It is important to move in His timing. Choosing to avoid or delay in the battle will hold off the glory move of revival and transformation that we all are believing and standing for. As spoken about in Chapter Ten, when Joshua did fight and possess the Promised Land they experienced rest in the land. At the writing of this book, I fully believe we are in a season when the Lord is awakening the church to warfare prayer yet again to see giants defeated in the land. *Lord, cause us to be obedient ones to take possession of the lands You have given as an inheritance.*

Prophesy and Decree His Word

As stated in Chapter Seven, to be a prophetic people we are not to give scripted prophetic prayers or answers to the warfare assignments we engage in, but prophecies, declarations, and decrees that are born in His presence, from His heart. Every city, land, and nation has its own calling and destiny. Hear me—God is a creative God. Most strategic prayer assignments are birthed or formed from a prophetic word released over a region or city. Truthfully, most of the assignments that I and our prayer network, SPAN, engage in are from prophetic words and revelations that the Lord speaks to us or that are spoken by prophets in prophetic gatherings. As shared in Chapter Eight in the assignment in Philadelphia, Mississippi, that entire assignment came from a prophetic vision the Lord revealed to me.

When He is speaking prophetic revelation and opening our spiritual eyes to see the demonic strongholds over regions, it is because He wants those who will pray, receive, and implement His strategy to see those entities defeated. If He is revealing these entities to leaders and intercessors who are ready to engage at this level, it is because He is giving you the assignment and authority to deal with it. I wonder how many warfare assignments have not been engaged in because the prophetic word and revelation from the Lord was not stewarded. So many people miss this key understanding in bringing breakthrough and transformation. Leaders in a region will go to a conference and prophets will minister the word of the Lord for the city and the region. Everyone in attendance is excited, but there must be the practice of the leaders and intercessors in the region praying into those words, asking the Lord for His Kingdom blueprint strategy concerning the prophetic word, and then putting the strategy in action. When prophetic words are released there will need to be prophetic-strategic intercessory assignments to see the fullness of the Word of the Lord manifested. We must partner with what He is saying and speaking.

As a reminder, in the glory, we have entered into the realm of His presence, revelation, and wisdom. We see as Jesus sees, hear as Jesus hears, and intercession is made from His anointed now word. I will state again, it is important when engaging in warfare prayer to not be trapped in the pattern of praying rote prayers.

Form a Strategy

We have stated before that satan is a strategist. Therefore, it is beneficial for us to learn how to be strategists. To be an army that is on offense and in a prepared mode to advance, strategy is key. This entails being ones who discover the enemy's schemes so he might not outwit us. Effectual strategy often involves what is termed informed intercession, so we are prepared to pray on site with insight. This is also referred to as spiritual mapping. This is the process of combining prophetic revelation that is received in His glory presence with the key history of a region. The two are then combined together to form a map of how to discern open doors to principalities in the region. A strategy is then implemented and engaged in to see these spirits defeated. Here are a few pointers to bring direction in understanding the history.

1. Who were the original inhabitants of the land and what happened to them? Who or how did they worship?

2. Why was the city established? Is there a history of corruption in the founding fathers or the government?

3. What were the foundational principles of the city? Were secret societies involved?

4. Is there trauma in the history of the region?

5. Was there bloodshed in the history of the land?

6. Was the city founded on Christian principles?

7. Is there evidence of corruption and greed in the government or economy of the city?

8. What are the righteous activities in the city that the Lord is blessing?

9. What are the spoken prophetic words over the region from which a strategy should be formed?

Pray in a Team

I will not belabor this point further as it has been mentioned in previous chapters. Remember, there are no lone rangers when praying at this level. To form a special ops glory-anointed team there are certain qualifications to be considered. The prayer warriors should be those who come to pray at the leading of the Holy Spirit. Ones who are open to the prophetic voice of the Lord. Ones who are mature and are not walking in known sin. They must be bold, unafraid, and in alignment with a local church or ministry.

Partner with Leaders in the Land

When working an assignment in regions it is beneficial to connect with leaders in the region. So what are the key things to remember when partnering together for breakthrough?

1. The leaders who are working with the special ops team need to be in unity with each other and with the team.

2. The leaders in the region as well as the team should have times of focused prayer, fasting, worship, intercession, and strategy leading into the assignment.

3. Scouting trips of those in the region should be implemented to gather research and information.

4. There needs to be a trained army in the region who will maintain the victory and continue to build, establish, and possess.

5. The leaders of the region should agree to be involved in the prayer assignment that is being formed.

6. Research should be completed and leaders in the region and the special ops team should be familiar with the history.

7. In prayer and intercession the strongmen over the region should to be identified and all participating prepared to break its hold.

ONSITE ENGAGEMENT

The following are a few directives of how to pray once you are on site. Again, for further teaching on how to engage in praying at this level, see *Authority to Tread*.

Repent for the Defilement

Repentance breaks the back of the enemy. Therefore, just as Nehemiah repented for the sins of his forefathers before initiating the rebuilding of the walls of Jerusalem, the same will need to occur in the land (see Neh. 1). This is often referred to as identificational repentance.

Break the Hold of the Principalities off of the Land

Many will often ask if we are to command a principality to leave. I believe Jesus is the best example to follow from Scripture. Let's look at how He addressed satan at the end of the temptation in the wilderness. "Then Jesus said to him, 'Go away, satan! For it is written and forever remains written, "You shall worship the Lord your God, and serve Him only"'" (Matt. 4:10 AMP). The Greek word for "go away" is *hupago*. It means to depart, leave, die, retire, depart this life (Strong's #G5217). It seems to me if Jesus in this strategic warfare confrontation commanded satan to leave, depart, die, then we too are able to do the same on the assignments He entrusts us with.

Release His Redemptive Purpose

Now is the time to speak restoration of the city to its original calling. Every city, region, and nation has been established by God for His purpose and plan. Seek the Lord for the reason the city has been established and begin to speak out and to cultivate His redemptive gift to the region.

Worship and Welcome His Glory to Fill the Land

Worship is one of the most powerful weapons of warfare. Your worship, your praise, your voice is a powerful instrument of warfare. You can bring the glory into your city, region, and nation with worship and praise. Once the strongholds have been defeated, release the worship to fill the empty void with the glory of the Lord. It is the same principle we practice in deliverance ministry. Once a house has been swept clean, it must be filled up so the strongman does not return with seven others making its latter condition worse than the former. The land must be filled with worship and praise to the Lord.

Prophesy and Decree the Now Word of the Lord

Now that the land is free, speak the Lord's prophetic destiny into the atmosphere. Agree with His now word for the region and begin to steward that word. Speak the promises He has given you from the Word. This might also include prophetic acts in and on the land.

Establish a Standard to Maintain the Victory

The leaders of the region must maintain the breakthrough and victory that has occurred. Sometimes this can be done through 24/7 worship. Other times it is through establishing an apostolic or prophetic presence in the region—prayer groups watching and guarding and not allowing the principalities to regain an entrance. This is where we must be on offense. Hold that victory, maintain, and begin to build.

SPAIN

As stated earlier in the book, we have been traveling to Spain and partnering with leaders Jose and Elba Lopez since 2004. On one assignment we prayed in Calasparra, the city in which Jose and Elba live. It is a region that for many years has been steeped in idol worship to an entity with the given name of la virgen de la esparanza—the virgin of hope. Idol worshipers crawl on their hands and knees up the 4,000-foot mountain to the temple cave. Upon arrival they crawl to the altar in front of the idol spilling their blood from their physical wounds. They believe this will bring assurance of salvation. Another ritual performed is the dedicating of children and infirmed family members to this entity by bringing miniature wax figurines of babies and body parts. The babies are hung by the neck with yarn. The children and sick relatives' names are hand-written on a note. It is heartbreaking that these worshipers believe these dedications bring life, when in actuality the exact opposite is true. This idol represents a spirit of death, and through years of these forms of worship a stronghold of death and suicide was welcomed in and enthroned over this region. The youth were committing suicide with the most common form being suicide by hanging.

We prayed and broke the spirit of death and witchcraft. Since this time of intercession the suicides stopped. To continue to see more freedom come and to maintain the victory, every Friday night for two years Jose and Elba's children and the youth of the church would lead worship to Jesus and share the truth of His love at the entry to the temple.

I returned three years later with another team and we prayed again. I was amazed to see what had transpired with the mountain that houses the temple cave. It had begun to crumble. The city government placed fencing along the sides in an attempt to hold it in place. We once again decreed death defeated and that a harvest would begin to come forth in Calasparra.

Following this time of prayer, those trapped in this worship, drug addicts, and families began to get saved. God's presence and glory began to show in tangible, undeniable moves in Jose and Elba's church. One newborn baby in the church became ill and died; Jose laid hands on her and she was resurrected. At the writing of this book she is ten years old.

The Lord spoke to Jose and Elba to hold a worship event in the city plaza to glorify Jesus on the same day that an ox-drawn cart brings a flower wreath offering to the virgin. In this ceremony, the ox pulls the cart through the city up the mountain and into the temple cave where the wreath is presented to the idol. An amazing occurrence happened during the praise celebration to Jesus. As soon as the ox-drawn cart hit the boundary line of the city, one of the oxen unexplainably dropped dead. No offering was made to the idol that year!

There is a river that runs next to the mountain and the virgin's temple. Twice the river has flooded to such an extent that it has risen to the top of that high mountain and flooded over into the area surrounding the cave. The foundation that is funding the worship location has now gone bankrupt. Not only are people being set free and saved, but the land is being set free. The Lord spoke to Jose and an elder in his church to purchase land on which they planted a peach and nectarine orchard. Within one year the trees outgrew the surrounding orchards which had already been in production for over 10 to 15 years. Their harvest yielded double what the other orchards were able to produce. They are now opening a business to have jams made from the peaches, which will include exporting abroad.

In the midst of this blessing, Jose and Elba's ministry has grown and is branching out across the nation of Spain. Along with their sons and daughter they are establishing another apostolic center in Murcia, Spain, and are launching a third work in Sevilla. Friends, I could continue to list more dramatic breakthroughs that have transpired and that are still transpiring. Writing this makes me want to shout a big, "Woohoo! Go God!"

GOD CAN SAVE A CITY AND A NATION

Friends, God does want to save and transform cities and nations. The following is a testament to the powerful encounters from the Welsh Revival in which Rees Howells was an intercessor. It was said that the presence and the power of the Holy Spirit was acknowledged. But often they had to pray out hindrances to move into the blessing of His manifested move and power. The two most consistent hindrances were disobedience and unforgiving hearts. But when obedience to the leading of the Holy Spirit was welcomed and the open and spoken confessions of Christ released, His blessings would come. Hymns were sung in one accord without a leader, but those in attendance could feel an unseen control leading them corporately. Noise and excitement was evident as they gathered, but it was due to the fact that people were being set free from bondages. What was occurring in the awakening and revival in the Church began to dramatically influence the city of Swansea. But some did not value this new move and chose to complain. One old preacher replied with a comment that I so love, "I prefer the noise of the city to the silence of the cemetery!"

Do we want dead cities, regions, and nations that are not spiritually alive or do we want awakened ones stirred to passion, revival, and tangible measures of transformation? I agree with C. Peter Wagner's statement placed at the opening of this chapter: "If individuals can be born again, why can't cities, made up of many individuals, be born again?" Friends, let's be city, region, and nation transformers bringing His Kingdom and glory into the uttermost parts of the earth.

CHAPTER TWELVE

ARISE, SHINE

*God, we've heard about all the glorious miracle you've
done for our ancestors in days gone by. They told us
about the ancient times, how by your power you drove
out the ungodly nations from this land, crushing all their
strongholds and giving the land to us. Now the people of
Israel cover the land from one end to the other, all because
of your grace and power! Our forefathers didn't win these
battles by their own strength or their own skill or strategy.
But it was through the shining forth of your radiant
presence and the display of your mighty power. You loved
to give them victory, for you took great delight in them.*
—Psalm 44:1-3 TPT

"It was through the shining forth of Your radiant presence and the display of Your mighty power. You loved to give them victory, for You took great delight in them." Do you hear the word of the Lord through David? His light that dispels darkness, His enlightened judgment, the light of His glory partnered with His power and strength of His military force is what He implemented to secure and give the children of Israel victory. And why did He give the victory? Because He was well pleased with, found favor, took great delight in, and loved them. Friends, this is the heavenly Father I love, worship, adore, and serve. Do you hear the word of the Lord? He loves to give victory.

In Chapter One, we began our study in this book by speaking of His glory and being vitally united to and abiding in Him. We have discussed in depth about authority, different realms of warfare that we engage at a personal level, and also in spheres of society, cities, regions, and nations. Now is the time to look at the first two words of Isaiah 60:1—*arise, shine*—and to hear the challenge that is being issued and the Kingdom inheritance that has been bestowed.

The Hebrew word for "arise" is *qum*. It means to abide, stand up, raise up, establish, raise up in opposition to a foe or an opponent, accomplish, strengthen, hold up, and establish (Strong's #H6965). Here we have arrived again at the abiding place, and from this place of surrender in His glory we stand up and rise up in opposition to a foe in order to accomplish, strengthen, hold up, and establish. The Hebrew word for shine is *or*. It means to give light; brighten; give sight; countenance of the face and eyes that shines with health, joy, peace; build a fire; set on fire; exude light; request favorable circumstances; and to bring relief from trouble and danger (Strong's #H215). We are not to be a beaten-up Body of believers, victimized by satan and his demonic army. But we are called ones whom the glory of the Lord rises upon in such a way that it is in virtual proximity to us. In other words, we are enveloped in His fire and glory and from there we pray, intercede, contend, and engage in warfare assignments to see His Kingdom come.

Isaiah goes on to prophesy, "For the darkness shall cover the earth and deep darkness the peoples; but the Lord shall rise upon you, and His glory shall be seen upon you" (Isa. 60:2). Even though darkness covers the earth and deep darkness the people, the Lord's glory will rise upon us and it will be seen on us. What does it signify when His glory is seen on you and me? It means to see, view, see vision, find delight, discover, give aid, selected, be present, experience, meet with advice, and to have an encounter with a military head just prior to a fight between hostile military parties. Wow! His glory being seen upon us carries prophetic revelation and a warrior anointing to encounter a military head before a fight in battle. What is the result of that battle between hostile military parties? "Nations shall come to your light and kings to the brightness of your rising" (Isa. 60:3). Nations, kings, and kingdoms are calling. They are seeking the light of His Kingdom and that dawning of a new day. This glory-anointed stance of a warrior brings such breakthrough that nations and kings will be transformed and returned to the brightness of the Lord. He is ready for a dawning of a new day. I believe the correct question is, are we ready for the dawning of a new day?

Mariano Riscajche is a pastor of a church in Almolonga, Guatemala, which is a village that has seen drastic Kingdom transformation since the 1980s. Ninety percent of the population is Christian, and this transformation is still occurring today. Much of this victory came when they engaged in warfare prayer against the stronghold of their village that was given ground through the worship of an idol by the name of maximon. Once they broke the power of the territorial spirit, they literally threw maximon out of the city. The city experienced great transformation. Mariano says that the miracle of Almolonga should not be unique at all: "Just as God did it here, it can happen everywhere in the world. What the Lord wants to do, in any place, is to show that, through His power, He can lead people to a better life."[1]

Hear and receive the promise that David scribed in Psalm 2:8: "Ask of Me, and I will give the nations for your inheritance." He is calling the awakened, surrendered ones to ask, contend, and believe. He is sending these anointed warriors with awakening and transformation in the sound of their voice—glory carriers who will go to the ends of the earth to those dark places where there is such a desperate need of His light, love, and Kingdom. Those who will arise and shine, intercede, prophesy, strategize, contend, bring breakthrough, transform, and possess.

GLORY ENCOUNTERS THAT IGNITE

As we begin to draw this book to a close, I want to share prophetic encounters that I have experienced in the past few months that I pray will encourage you as you read, confirm what is being shared in this book, and draw you into a season of being impassioned for victorious warfare.

To be honest, in the season of receiving these revelations and words I was in such need of experiencing more of Him. There was a longing to encounter Him. This season I had been in had proven difficult at times. However, the Lord never wastes a season in our lives and causes all things to work for good. This longing was pressing and pushing me into a time of going deeper into heavenly encounters. As I am writing, I feel you may be in this same place—feeling pressed, but the pressing has pushed you into seeking and wanting more of Him, causing you to go beyond to places with Him you might not have been before. Allow me to share a personal experience that happened just recently for me, Greg, and several of the prayer leaders in our ministry.

The Lord impressed upon us to go to Wales, to spend time in the Bible college that was founded by Rees Howells. Not only were we to spend time there, but we were to pray in the chapel and the Blue Room where all the years of history-making, Holy Spirit-empowered intercession had occurred. The Lord was speaking to go back to the place of the anointing that had been so mightily used by the Lord when I was called to intercession for the nations. Go back to that place because there was more that He wanted us to receive in that mantle of intercession. It felt as if a holy, glorious impartation would occur. One that would take us beyond, causing us to go higher and deeper in the impartation of our calling.

As stated previously, Greg and I went together in January 2017. We spent three days in the chapel praying, interceding, and dedicating our lives and our ministry to the Lord. It was a moment between the two of us and the Lord when He spoke so clearly to us personally and for the ministry we lead. It was a glorious, holy, sacred time of surrendered consecration. He ignited the passion for the nations again and sealed it in beautiful glory encounters with Him.

Then in March we took a small group of prayer leaders in our prayer network. We were welcomed and given two full days in the chapel, were involved in an intercessory prayer time for the nations in the Blue Room, and visited Pisgah Chapel and Moriah Chapel where the Welsh Revival occurred through Evan Roberts. I have to admit what transpired for us in those four days in Wales was beyond words. But I am going to share some of the things that I feel will spur you to hunger for more of Him and impart faith to enter into a fresh encounter of His fire and glory.

There is an anointing that we encountered in our prayer times that I am going to attempt to describe. This is not shared to make it sound as if we are special because of what transpired, but to encourage you to move into an abiding, surrendered place that causes a rising up to purpose, destiny, and victory. His magnificent glory came into our prayer times. It was tangible and holy, a glorious heavenly presence so real that it causes you to want to surrender all you are, to lay down all that you have, and consecrate everything to Him. A presence where groans begin to rise in the room, "Lord, I want more of You. I need more of You. I surrender all to You. Jesus, we want more of You."

When we entered this place of consecrated surrender He met with us. There was an expansion in the Spirit that occurred for each person in that divine encounter moment. We caught the glory wave of intercession within the history and the sound of those walls from years of nation-shifting intercession. The glory wave of the Holy Spirit swept us up into the atmosphere of heaven. But the beauty was as we were swept up into the atmosphere of heaven, the atmosphere of the glory and heaven met us in that prayer chapel. We were in a womb of intercession that had captured and carried within its memory all of the intercession across the generations. It was a time of synergy, a converging point. We were one with Him and eternity in that prayer room. And as we pressed into a place of complete adoration and abandonment to Him, He expanded us to think so far beyond ourselves, sweeping us into a passion for the nations that was beautiful, glorious, full of immense holiness and joy. The nations became the cry of our hearts. It was as if our intercession was a bowl being tipped out for the nations. I am undone all over again typing this. The lead intercessor of the Bible college had joined us in the chapel and at one point she began to pray, sing, and prophesy. Here is one word she delivered in this holy moment.

> This is special, oh this is special! I see a window of heaven open and oil just pouring down—there is a pouring forth into this time right now. And I just see a portal and it's open right now in the center of this room. And it's pouring forth oil and the wine. He's pouring it in the center of this room right now. And it is just moving, coming toward us! It's spreading over the whole room. Oh, the oil and the wine. By faith we stand in it. By faith we lay (prostrate) in it. Oh, Holy Spirit You make all this possible. Oh Lord, for the healing of the nations. We are at the dawn of an awakening. We are at the dawn of a breaking, a breaking of the Spirit of the Lord. The latter rain. The latter rain. Take your places now. Take your places. You are vessels of honor, vessels filled with My power and My Spirit. Stand before Me, consecrated. There

are amazing things I will do. We are at the dawn of an awakening and the dawn of a breaking. Be ready, be expectant!

Friends, I feel this word was not just for those of us who were in the chapel at this moment, but I feel this is what is available for all of those who will come to this moment of consecration of pulling themselves into an undivided time where He is your only focus and intent. There is a new and fresh holy fire and glory outpouring that He is bringing for those who will hunger, thirst for, and seek after Him.

Allow me to share further insight concerning Moses and Joshua and this tent of meeting as a scriptural example where we see men anointed in the glory who shaped history of people and lands.

> *Inside the Tent of Meeting, the Lord would speak to Moses face to face, as one speaks to a friend. Afterward Moses would return to the camp, but the young man who assisted him, Joshua son of Nun, would remain behind in the Tent of Meeting* (Exodus 33:11 NLT).

God spoke to Moses face to face as a friend. Moses was truly abiding, and Joshua was invited to be in that atmosphere. But look at Joshua's position during what would be for him a spiritual awakening season. When Moses left the tent, Joshua would remain in the place of consecration. The place that carried with it the cost of pulling away and intentional, dedicated time to meet with Him face to face as a friend. And in this tent of meeting, in this place of consecration, Joshua was anointed in the glory with authority to take action, contend, war, and possess. He was the one anointed as the glory carrier to war against enemies and to possess for the Kingdom. If we desire to contend and possess then we must come to the place of the tent of meeting and be filled fresh and new to advance. Friends, hear this truth—the enemy knows and fears those who come to the tent of meeting, the place of consecration, to ascend in heaven where you become one on fire with His Kingdom purposes.

Some might be contemplating and thinking, "Yes, this did occur, but this was in the Old Testament and for the season Moses and Joshua were in to deliver the children of Israel and possess the Promised Land. But what about now?" First, there is still a promised land we are to possess. Jesus stated, "Blessed are the meek, for they will inherit the earth" (Matt. 5:5 NIV). And another directive given by Jesus: "Go and make disciples of all nations" (Matt. 28:19 NIV). And the beauty is He sent someone better to guide, help, and empower us in this process.

Let's look again at Acts 2 when the Holy Spirit came at Pentecost. We've talked about the 120 and that each of us can become a burning bush, set aflame and on fire for Him. When the tongues of fire were distributed on each of them, they received their new languages. This outpouring of fire also brought ecstatic joy, eloquence of language, a boldness to speak of and to do great exploits for the Kingdom of God. To be filled signifies we become swollen or fat with Him. Make the time to surrender and encounter Him. The result will be an expansion in the Spirit and moving into a place of thinking beyond yourself. When you move beyond yourself He will speak intercessory burdens for the people, spheres, and lands you are called to. This is the army that will have victory. This is the army that will count the cost and cry out, "Lord, here am I, use me!" This is the army that humbles itself before the Lord and is anointed to see the schemes of the enemy defeated and destroyed. This is the awakened army full of His fire and glory. Bold ones burning for Him. Fearless ones who cause darkness to tremble and to flee. This is the army that will gain personal victory. This is the army that will possess gates of influence. This is the army that will transform cities, regions, and nations. This is the army that will have the victory.

THE ARMY OF THE LORD IS MARCHING IN CADENCE

In 2007, I had a vision of the army of the Lord. The army was standing in line and file and rank, but every soldier was standing in position asleep. It was not an awakened army. Beginning in October of 2017, I prophetically began to hear and see this army again. In the vision, the Lord showed me it is a new season and I am now seeing this army in a new way. The army is standing in file and rank. They are fully awakened and they are marching in place, in step and unity in a strong military cadence. In the vision, they are awaiting the announcement of their Commander in Chief to advance. The longer the army marches in place, the stronger the cadence, the sound of the cadence, and step of the march becomes. It is increasing in intentional focus and authority. That place of tension for the shout of release from their commander to advance. Suddenly, the sound of the general's voice echoes a decree in the atmosphere, "Advance and possess!" This united, anointed, and prepared army begins to advance with the fullness of Kingdom expression into victory in a battle.

What Does This Mean Personally?

As I have been meditating on this revelation and pressing into times of intercession with the Holy Spirit, I stated above, I sense many of you are in a season where you are doing the same. Some pressing in because of hurt and betrayal. Some desperately pressing in because of a trauma or pain or loss. Some pressing in because words that have been spoken against you by others which is causing confusion with what you feel the Lord has spoken to you concerning personal direction. Some pressing in because you have been in that wilderness and you are so hungry for more of Him and desire to experience Him in His glory, His presence and His love. Some are pressing in because you feel Him drawing you to go beyond. You may be pressing in because you hear the call in the distance. You are in this place of tension. Waiting for the command to advance. I, too, have been pressing into

Him, and I want to share the remainder of this word which I believe will encourage you.

I Will Not Leave You!

We are in an Issachar season to know the anointing we are to move in. Even when others might not go with you through the doors in the new season, stay close to Him. Be with the Lord as Elisha was to Elijah. When Elijah knew he was being taken up, Elisha repeatedly told Elijah, "I will not leave you!" When the translations of these words are looked at closely, Elisha spoke in a language that can almost be translated, "You cannot get rid of me, I am stuck to you like glue!" In this season of your life, be stuck to our Father, Jesus, and Holy Spirit like glue. You will not be able to go through the new door or your gate of influence in your own strength, but in and through Him.

Joy in Our Words, Joy in Our Lives, Joy to Produce Life!

Joy will be found and restored and re-fired in our personal lives, situations, and prayer assignments. Joy will be found in our words. The truth is that what we believe and speak out becomes the prophecy by which we live out our lives. We become our own personal prophets! Allow the Lord to restore His joy, truth, and love to fill the words of your mouth. Pull away and connect with Holy Spirit. Welcome His life, fire, glory, joy, and love to come to those dry places. He is the one who will release the joy to bring flesh, sinew, and life to those dry and dead bones. *It is time for those lifeless and dry bones to receive resurrection life.* A key understanding to grab hold of and to operate in—the greatest lovers make the greatest warriors because it gives us a cause to fight from and to fight for. What He loves—people, harvest, the lost, cities, regions, and nations—we will fight for with Him, and what He hates—meaning the enemy's dark schemes of evil and his dark army—we will war against, not for victory but from victory. And His angel armies will be sent to partner with us. Weariness is breaking off the army. Be encouraged in His joy and life!

Knowledge of His Glory

He is moving in glory waves. He is bringing us into personal encounters. I continue to hear Him say, "It's time for a consecration, glory realm, altar encounter with Him." He is bringing us into a moment of an altar encounter where, in this place of encountering Him, waves of His glory will come into emotions, thoughts, beliefs to move us through into this season He has designed and destined for us. A holiness consecration. From this place of surrender on the altar of consecration, there will be an army that will rise up. An anointing from that Holy Spirit abiding place to cause us to rise from the altar of consecration into the position of His strength, full of authority, armed in the glory, and ready to advance into the new. An overcomer's mindset! A victorious mindset! It is a season of the knowledge of the glory of the Lord coming alive to the Ekkleisa and the earth. You may have already risen and are marching in sync with the King of kings and the Lord of lords. I want to encourage each of us to make time for the moment or the altar of consecration and enter into this new cadence of movement, and you too will be one to release the sound of the army marching in sync and cadence with Him.

In Closing

Friends, this I do know. We are to be His ambassadors directing the world to Him. He is a faithful God. His promises are true. He never leaves us or forsakes us. He is the Alpha, Omega, the Beginning and the End. He is the Risen Savior. He is Truth. He is the Deliverer and Healer. He is Love. He is Righteous Judge full of justice. He is Holiness. He is Majesty.

After that I saw heaven opened, and behold, a white horse [appeared]! The One Who was riding it is called Faithful (Trustworthy, Loyal, Incorruptible, Steady) and True, and He passes judgment and wages war in righteousness (holiness, justice, and uprightness). His eyes [blaze] like a flame

*of fire, and on His head are many kingly crowns (diadems);
and He has a title (name) inscribed which He alone knows
or can understand. He is dressed in a robe dyed by dipping in
blood, and the title by which He is called is The Word of God.
And the troops of heaven, clothed in fine linen, dazzling and
clean, followed Him on white horses. From His mouth goes
forth a sharp sword with which He can smite (afflict, strike)
the nations; and He will shepherd and control them with a
staff (scepter, rod) of iron. He will tread the winepress of the
fierceness of the wrath and indignation of God the All-Ruler
(the Almighty, the Omnipotent). And on His garment (robe)
and on His thigh He has a name (title) inscribed, King of
kings and Lord of lords* (Revelation 19:11-16 AMPC).

He is King of kings and Lord of lords! He rides on a white horse. The earth is the Lord's and the fullness thereof. All of heaven is filled with His glory and resounds with praise—holy are You, Lord! This is the Kingdom of the glorious King we serve. It is time to arise and shine! We have been given a rich inheritance in the Kingdom. Through encountering Him in all His glory, we are marked with a responsibility to stand in this dark world, to see captives set free, the lost saved, people healed, cities and lands freed from the grip of principalities and ushered into Kingdom transformation. This is your call to arms; it is time to be anointed and empowered to war from the glory realm. Our prayers, our actions, our willingness to contend against darkness and evil have the power to heal the past and shape the future. Let the voice and authority of the glory-anointed Ekklesia arise and resound.

NOTES

INTRODUCTION

1. C. Peter Wagner, *Confronting the Powers: How the New Testament Church Experienced the Power of Strategic-Level Spiritual Warfare* (Ventur, CA: Regal Books, 1996), 121.

CHAPTER ONE: ENTER THE GLORY REALM

1. Alice Smith, *Beyond the Veil: Entering Intimacy with God Through Prayer* (Ventura, CA: Regal Books, 1997), 155.

2. Norman Grubb, *Rees Howells, Intercessor* (Fort Washington, PA: CLC Publications, 2016), 65-66.

CHAPTER TWO: ENROLLED IN THE MOST POWERFUL ARMY IN THE UNIVERSE

1. Eddie Smith, *Spiritual Advocates: How to Plead for Justice, Stand in the Gap, and Make a Difference in the World by Praying for Others* (Lake Mary, FL: Charisma House, 2008), 81.

2. C. Peter Wagner, *Warfare Prayer: What the Bible Says About Spiritual Warfare* (Shippensburg, PA: Destiny Image, 2009), 51.

3. Eddie Smith, *Making Sense of Spiritual Warfare* (Bloomington, MN: Bethany House, 2008), 73.

4. Operation Rescue, "Tiller's License at Stake as KSBHA Launches New Abortion Investigation," October 4, 2007, https://www.operationrescue .org/archives/tiller%e2%80%99s-license-at-stake-as-ksbha-launches-new -abortion-investigation/.

5. Isabel Hernández, "Meet the Man Who Started the Illuminati," *National Geographic,* November 01, 2016, https://www.nationalgeographic .com/archaeology-and-history/magazine/2016/07-08/profile-adam -weishaupt-illuminati-secret-society/.

CHAPTER FIVE: ASSIGNED FOR VICTORY

1. C. Peter Wagner, *Warfare Prayer,* 111.

2. Jon Bloom, "Lay Aside the Fear of Man," *Desiring God,* September 16, 2016, https://www.desiringgod.org/articles/lay-aside-the-fear-of-man.

3. John Bevere, *Honor's Reward: How to Attract God's Favor and Blessing* (New York, New York: Faith Words, 2007), 16.

4. "U.S. Army Values," April 6, 2018, https://www.army.mil/values.

CHAPTER EIGHT: KEYS OF AUTHORITY

1. C. Peter Wagner, *Warfare Prayer,* 213-232.

2. "Mississippi Band of Choctaw Indians Tribal Chief Phyliss J. Anderson," *Forbes Magazine*; February 27, 2012.

3. Dean Briggs, *Ekklesia Rising: The Authority of Christ in Communities of Contending Prayer* (Champion Press: Kindle Edition), 169-170.

CHAPTER NINE: ENGAGING PERSONAL VICTORY

1. Fruitful Sermons, "Jerusalem Conference - Kathryn Kuhlman, 1974," YouTube, March 01, 2015, https://www.youtube.com/ watch?v=iL2xx9Jm7vE.

CHAPTER TEN: POSSESSING YOUR GATES OF INFLUENCE

1. Cindy Jacobs, *Possessing the Gates of the Enemy: A Training Manual for Militant Intercession* (Ann Arbor, Michigan: Chosen Books, 2009), 15.

2. E.M. Bounds, *Purpose in Prayer* (New York, NY: Fleming H. Revell Company, 1920), 9-11, 20.

3. Smith Wigglesworth, *The Anointing of His Spirit* (Ventura, CA: Gospel Light, 1994), 159.

4. John Wesley, *A Plain Account of Christian Perfection* (Kansas City, MO: Beacon Hill Press, 1966), 106.

5. S.D. Gordon, *Quiet Talks on Prayer* (New York, NY: Fleming H. Revell Company, 1904), 19.

CHAPTER ELEVEN: GLORY IN THE LAND

1. Jacobs, *Possessing the Gates of the Enemy*, 217.

CHAPTER TWELVE: ARISE, SHINE

1. Sarah Pollak, The Christian Broadcasting Network, 2007.

About Rebecca Greenwood

Rebecca Greenwood cofounded Christian Harvest International and Strategic Prayer Apostolic Network, which ministers to the nations through prophecy, prophetic intercession, transformational spiritual warfare prayer, and teaching of the Word of God. Over the past 24 years, she has traveled to and ministered in 45 nations and participated in and led spiritual warfare prayer journeys to 34 countries in which measurable transformations have been realized. Rebecca and her husband, Greg, reside in Colorado Springs, Colorado, and they have three beautiful daughters.

OTHER BOOKS BY REBECCA GREENWOOD

Authority to Tread: An Intercessor's Guide to
Strategic-Level Spiritual Warfare

Breaking the Bonds of Evil: How to Set People
Free from Demonic Oppression

The Power of a Godly Mother

Destined to Rule: Spiritual Strategies for Advancing the Kingdom of God

Let Our Children Go: Steps to Free Your Child from
Evil Influence and Demonic Harassment

Your Kingdom Come: Encouraged to Intercede

Contributor to *Understanding Spiritual Warfare: Four Views*

Defeating Strongholds of the Mind: A Believer's Guide to Breaking Free

Are you ready to join the Army of the Lord?

Enroll in our Spiritual Warfare Online School taught
by Becca Greenwood!

Go to: spanprayer.org/spiritual-warfare-online-school